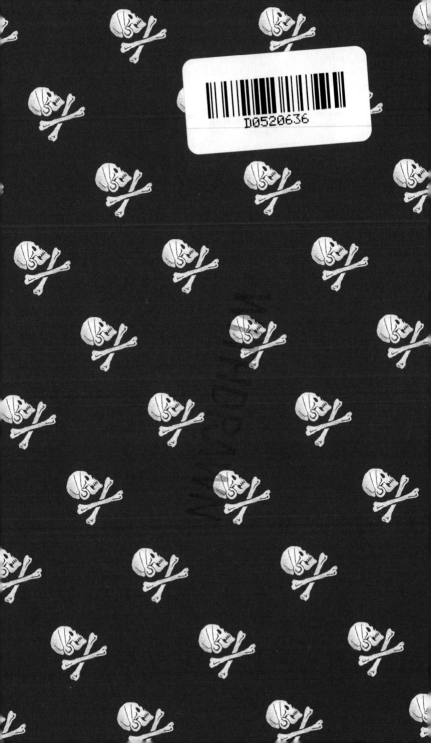

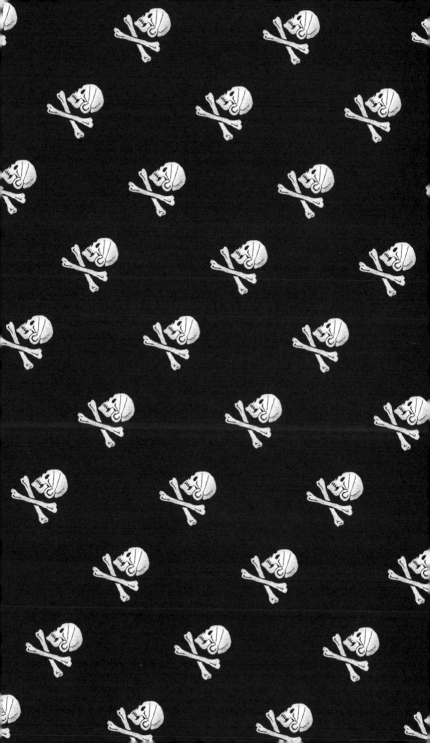

PIRATE

Stephen Turnbull

PIRATE

THE BUCCANEER'S
UNOFFICIAL MANUAL

122 illustrations

Thames & Hudson

In loving memory of Marilyn Knowles

On the cover: Captain Edward Teach, better known as Blackbeard. Hulton Archive/ Getty Images

Pirate: The Buccaneer's (Unofficial) Manual © 2018 Thames & Hudson Ltd
Text © 2018 Stephen Turnbull

First published in 2018 in the United States of America by Thames & Hudson Inc., 500 Fifth Avenue, New York, New York 10110

www.thamesandhudsonusa.com

Library of Congress Control Number 2017945554

ISBN 978-0-500-25223-9

Printed and bound in China by Shanghai Offset Printing Products Ltd

Contents

So you want to be a pirate?

Think very carefully about it!

Are you surprised by what I have just written? Well, let me introduce myself, my young friend, and then perhaps you will understand what I mean by thinking very carefully about it. I am not going to tell you my name, for two reasons. First, because I am wanted by every excise man and local watch from the Spanish Main to the Barbary Coast. Second, because if I was to tell you who I really am you would be so terrified that you wouldn't want to read this book... and we don't want that, do we?

So think carefully before you turn the page, because this book will tell you, like no other book ever written, how to become a pirate and then how to live a long and successful life without ending up hanging by your neck from the yardarm. This is because it is a book that has been written by someone who was once young like you, and now, well... let's say that I have had something of a career! I have lost one eye and one leg but none of my wits, and I have learned a thing or two that I now want to pass on to you.

Note, however, my young friend, that this book is not based solely on what I have seen and done all by myself. I have met a wide mixture of honest sailors and black-hearted villains from all over this wicked world, and it is their wisdom too that I include within this book. You will learn not only about pirate life among the buccaneers of the Caribbean, but of the pirates and privateers of North America, the Muslim fleets of the Barbary Coast and the great bloodthirsty crews of China and Japan. Some of these men were very well educated and wrote journals that described in minute detail what the pirate life was really like for them. I have used their insights here, so you will find all the information you need to be a successful pirate. Every one of them has something valuable to teach us!

I have also spoken to men who served directly under the most famous pirates of them all. When my own father was young he sailed under the famous Bartholomew Roberts. 'Black Bart', as everyone called him, was blasted to smithereens half a century ago. It was a nasty end, but at least he cheated the hangman. During his career he was so notorious that when Black Bart died the government called him 'the last of the pirates' and told everyone that the days of piracy were over. Are they really a thing of the past? Read this book, my young friend, and let people decide for themselves if they have seen the last of the pirates!

Written in the Year of Our Lord 1793
in the Reign of His Majesty King George III

NOTE: The above letter 'X', being the mark of the author,
has been authenticated by reliable witnesses, all of whom have
now been shot dead as a precautionary measure.

I

Pírates and You

What is a pirate? The word can mean different things to different people. If you ask any passer-by you meet on the King's highway, they will probably tell you that a pirate is a wicked seafarer who attacks ships or raids towns, who unquestionably deserves to be hung, drawn and quartered. And indeed many pirates do end their brief careers by meeting the executioner. So why do so many people risk their lives that way, when they could serve His Majesty the King with pride as sailors in the navy instead? The short answer is 'money – and lots of it'. That is what being a pirate is really all about, and to get your hands on as much loot as possible, you must be a member of a pirate crew, and sail on a pirate ship. You could even have a pirate lair, hidden somewhere on a pirate island.

So that's clear. Or is it? The trouble is that many of the people that are commonly called pirates would never call themselves one. Take, for example, the interesting old seafarer Basil Ringrose, who lived from 1653 until 1686 and sailed as a ship's surgeon under Captain Bartholomew Sharpe. Ringrose described in his journal becoming very cross when he and his fellow sailors were classed as pirates, even though, of course, they were doing the very things that pirates always did. Instead he called himself a 'buccaneer', a title he was very proud of.

»→ The native Caribbean islanders' *buccan*, or *boucan* – a type of open grill – gave the buccaneers their name. The French settlers of Hispaniola smoked meat on the *buccan* to sell to passing ships.

'Buccaneer' comes from the French *boucanier*, and originally referred to hunters who had settled on the Caribbean island of Hispaniola and lived on wild pigs. They smoked the meat by cutting the flesh into strips and grilling it slowly over a wood fire, preserving it so that they could eat in times of scarcity. The grill was called the *boucan*, and so the hunters became known as *boucaniers* – 'users of the boucan' – by the passing sailors who stopped to buy the smoked meat for their long voyages. Life on the island was tough, so the *boucaniers* had to be strong and warlike to survive at all, and it was not long before these hardy men were being recruited by the English colonists of Jamaica – who Anglicized their names in the process – in their fight against the Spanish. By 1655, these private buccaneer armies had chased the last of the Spanish troops from the island, but they didn't stop there, realizing that from their Jamaican stronghold they could make a pretty penny by raiding the Spanish galleons that passed nearby. The treasure they captured went to their employers, who paid them handsomely in return. 'Buccaneering', as they called it, took off.

Attacking Spanish galleons to steal their treasure? That sounds a lot like piracy, doesn't it? Yet the buccaneers did not regard themselves as pirates because they did not steal treasure for themselves. Instead they worked for others, usually their own governments, and received official permission to carry out their raids. Quite often this took the form of a written contract called a 'Letter of Marque'. This vital piece of paper would be shown to anyone who dared to call a buccaneer a pirate,

let alone tried to arrest them. This scheme was nothing new; hundreds of seafarers had worked the system for centuries, known as 'privateers' because they were officially licensed to carry out attacks against enemy shipping using their own vessels – their private property. As far back as 1243, King Henry III of England issued

🏃 This illustration from Captain Johnson's *General History of the Robberies and Murders of the most notorious Pyrates* imagines the pirate not as a noble privateer, but a menacing villain. In the distance lurks the certain prospect of the gallows for the fearsome pirate brandishing her cutlass.

a contract to two men, Adam Robernolt and William le Sauvage, to 'annoy our enemies by sea and land' – that is, to raid French ships in the English Channel. In return for this freedom, all they had to do was share half their plunder with the King. By the seventeenth century, then, the legitimacy of private warfare on behalf of a ruler was well established, so the new buccaneers fitted in very neatly. In time, privateers came to be contracted by commercial companies as well as monarchs, particularly in the American colonies of New England, on the north-east coast. For example, Clark & Nightingale, a firm based in Providence, Rhode Island, specializing in slaves and sugar, sponsored privateers to target British shipping in 1780.

So if privateers and buccaneers spend their time raiding ships, what makes a pirate any different? Well, I think you can guess the answer. Privateers and buccaneers *claim* that they are attacking and raiding on behalf of someone else, while as a pirate you will make no secret of the fact that you are out for yourself, and so will be universally regarded as a criminal. If you are caught, you will go to prison and might well be hanged. The pirate life isn't quite so romantic after all, is it?

'So can I be a buccaneer or a privateer instead of a pirate?' I hear you ask. Well, I have to be quite frank about this and say that your ultimate fate might not be very different. Yes, your Letter of Marque will show quite clearly that you have been officially commissioned to attack the ships of enemy nations – but to those foreign authorities, of course, you are a pirate pure and simple, and if they catch you then you will suffer the same consequences as if you were just a common pirate operating on your own. It's all a matter of perspective, the general

↟ Francis Drake was the picture of an English gentleman, and a hero in the eyes of the British public. He was not viewed so favourably by the Spanish crews he attacked for the riches they carried across the seas.

attitude being: 'my pirates are privateers; your privateers are pirates!' Just think of the famous Sir Francis Drake, one of the first so-called 'Sea Dog' privateers of England. Drake sailed on his most famous voyage from 1577 to 1580, becoming the first English captain to circumnavigate the globe (but not the first: the Portuguese sailor Ferdinand Magellan beat him to it). It was an eventful trip: he lost four of his five ships to bad weather; executed a subordinate for allegedly plotting a mutiny; raided various Spanish ports; and captured a fine Spanish vessel loaded with treasure. A delighted Queen Elizabeth immediately knighted him upon his return – but if the Spanish had caught him, he would have been hanged as a pirate. In England he was a great hero; in Spain, he was a villain. Amusingly, Her

 Woodcut of Sir Francis Drake landing at the River Plate (Río de la Plata) estuary in South America. Drake reached the Plate in 1578, in the early stages of his circumnavigation of the world in the *Golden Hind*. Drake would later die at sea, off the coast of Panama, aged 54.

Majesty the Queen affectionately called Drake her 'pirate'. So perhaps it's not such an insult after all...

It isn't just the English that want to have it both ways. Around the time of the buccaneers, we begin reading stories about famous French corsairs (the French word for a privateer), such as René Duguay-Trouin, who raided English ships on behalf of the French monarch. To the English he was a pirate, and to the French he was a hero – you see a familiar pattern emerges... The term 'corsair', incidentally, was also used for the Muslim crews of the Barbary Coast fleets and the Christian Knights of Malta, who had their own choice of legitimate targets – usually each other – and called each other pirates.

To complicate matters even further, there are some men who will serve whatever nation they choose, just as long as they get paid – the

↟ A sea battle between Italian galleys and Barbary ships in the Mediterranean. Both sides thought they were in the right, and called their opponents pirates.

naval equivalent of mercenaries. They will call themselves privateers, but there is nothing loyal or patriotic about them. One such operator, Edward Coxere, once compiled a long list of his various employers over the years – 'I served the Spaniards against the French, then the Hollanders against the English', and so on... Coxere was happy to go raiding for whoever would compensate him most generously. In fact, he served so many different nations that most of the world called him a pirate, whatever he might have fancied himself. The medieval pirate Eustace the Monk, who lived during the reign of King John in the twelfth century – making him one of the first privateers to operate in the English Channel – was similarly self-serving, abandoning the French monastery he had called home to pursue the pirate life. Betraying his homeland, he was employed by the English king to attack French shipping, and was so successful that it was rumoured that he was a magician who could make his ship invisible. But before long, Eustace grew so confident in his abilities that he attacked anyone who came along, making him a pirate in everyone's eyes. He antagonized the English Crown further by falling out with his once grateful king, and when John's successor, King Henry III, declared war on France, Eustace joined a French fleet sent to invade England. Eustace's ship was boarded by English sailors, and he was rewarded for his lack of patriotic spirit by being arrested and beheaded.

Pirate, privateer, corsair, buccaneer... whichever label you most identify with, there will always be someone somewhere in the world who regards you as a dastardly villain, so you might as well accept that you are a pirate, and that your future will lie somewhere between being knighted by a queen and being hanged by a king.

A short history of piracy

Piracy has been around as long as anyone can remember. It is a fact of life that when one person is trying to make an honest living, there will be another who wants to steal it from them. Now, consider that most trade between countries is carried out by ships sailing on the sea. Pirates have realized how vast the sea is, and have concluded that they are unlikely to be caught – once their crime is committed, they can simply sail on, hunting out a safe haven in which to enjoy the spoils of their efforts. And so, pirates have always existed; there is not a patch of sea on this great planet that has not seen pirates at some time in its history.

I once found an ancient Greek vase with a most intriguing design that showed pirates attacking honest merchant ships, but the battle looks very different from anything you are likely to experience yourself. The Greek pirate ship was propelled by oars along with one sail, with an eye painted on either side of the bows (the forward-facing part of a ship's hull). This type of ship is called a galley; you can still see oared ships today in the Mediterranean, where conditions are suitable for rowing. But you won't see modern oared ships attacking their prey in the same way that the ancient Greek pirates did. They built an iron ram into the bow of their vessel, and would just row up as fast as they could and bash into their target. The massive impact would hole the ship and disable it, even sinking it in time. Not surprisingly, the peaceful merchants of the Mediterranean soon began to hit back – the Phoenicians, themselves impressive seafarers, developed war galleys with rams of their own to sink the pirate ships.

⚡ The interior of this ancient Greek pot depicts the oared ships favoured by those who sailed in the calm waters of the Aegean Sea, where windpower alone could not be relied on.

Pirates even barged into the mythology of the ancient Greeks. One myth tells how the god Dionysus, the deity of wine and fertility, was captured by pirates, but not for long – the god magically changed himself into a fierce lion and punished his captors by transforming them all into dolphins. This story may have been based on the efforts of Alexander the Great (356–323 BC) to clear the pirates from the seas that he supposedly controlled.

Such battles played out in the waters of the ancient Middle East over the course of many hundreds of years. King Sennacherib, ruler of the Neo-Assyrian Empire from 705 to 682 BC, waged war against the pirates who raided his territory in what we now call the Persian Gulf. King Shapur II of Persia (AD 309–379) had the same problem in the same area many centuries later, and earned a reputation for retaliating with great ferocity, being said to have pierced holes into the shoulders of captured pirates and roped them together as prisoners.

The ancient Romans were also plagued by pirates. While the Roman Empire was still young, the important port of Delos, an island in the Greek Cyclades archipelago, was already a thriving pirate base where illicit traders openly sold slaves and loot. The Romans turned a blind eye to this until 67 BC, when pirates began to target their grain imports. The vital cereals were brought in large, slow vessels that were easy prey for determined pirates, whose raids threatened to cause starvation in the great city of Rome. A major operation conducted by sea and on land, led by Pompey the Great, succeeded in eliminating most of the marauders – but Pompey's own son, Sextus Pompeius (67–35 BC), received help from pirates in his (ultimately unsuccessful) naval campaign against his rival Octavian.

Slightly unusual were the Muslim pirates of the North African coast along the southern shore of the Mediterranean, known as the Barbary Coast. The name is derived from the Berber people who lived there. Kemal Reis, the first Barbary corsair, operated on behalf of the Ottoman Empire, a great power stretching across the Middle East and North Africa with its capital at Constantinople, Turkey.* This was a time when Christian and Muslim forces were at war. The corsairs were asked to help defend the Muslim stronghold of Granada in Spain, and led some successful raids against Christian ports. The corsairs established bases along the North African coast, such

* This wall relief from the Assyrian palace at Nineveh shows the oared warships commanded by Sennacherib, probably built by Phoenicians, the Assyrians' sea-faring neighbours.

* NOTE FROM THE EDITOR: Constantinople is now called Istanbul.

as at Bougie and on the island of Djerba. Using galleys not unlike those of the ancient Greeks, the Barbary corsairs rammed ships and took captives. The richer prisoners were ransomed; the poorer ones became slaves, forced to row the pirate ships. The mirror image of the Barbary corsairs were the Christian Knights of Malta. Just like the Crusaders before them, the Knights saw themselves as holy warriors; but so did the corsairs. The two groups fought fiercely against each other for many centuries.

Pirates are best known for accosting their victims on the open sea, but in many parts of the world raids against ships were launched from coastal hideaways. The Adriatic Sea, which separates Italy from the Balkans (see p. 23), is quite peaceful nowadays, but in the twelfth and thirteenth centuries Omis, a small harbour in Croatia, sheltered a band of pirates so fierce and powerful that even the mighty fortified city of Dubrovnik had to make deals with them. The town is built on a narrow gulf between huge cliffs, so the pirates favoured a sleek type of ship called a *sagittas* (arrow) that could quickly withdraw or lie in wait. They would attack anyone who passed by,

↯ Map of the Barbary Coast along North Africa during piracy's Golden Age.

raiding galleys travelling from Venice, Kotor, Split and even some owned by the Pope himself, but Venice started taking over the Adriatic during the fifteenth century and soon cracked down on this illegal activity.

At about the same time, the pirate crews of the Far East, known by their victims as *wako*, regularly raided coastal communities. The first syllable of their name, 'wa', is the ancient name given by the inhabitants of China and Korea to Japan, which shows clearly where the victims believed their tormentors had come from, but piracy in the Far East was by no means solely a Japanese occupation. By the mid-sixteenth century, individual pirate bands had acquired a decidedly cosmopolitan character: huge gangs made up of Chinese, Korean and even Portuguese pirates. Some of the most influential pirate leaders were renegade Chinese who sailed from bases on Japanese islands to terrorize their fellow countrymen under the convenient anonymity of *wako*, landing Japan with the blame. There are many stories about *wako* attacking ships, but most of the time they raided ashore, launching massive assaults on the coastal towns of China and Korea. Armies of as many as 3,000 *wako* are known to have been involved in such operations. Sometimes they captured slaves, and they also targeted ships carrying rice along rivers and coastlines.

There was also considerable pirate activity within Japan itself. The large stretch of water that divides Japan's main islands of Honshu, Kyushu and Shikoku is known as the Inland Sea, and the numerous small islands and inlets within it served as safe havens for any samurai general who fancied taking to the sea. The *kaizoku*, the domestic warrior pirates of the Inland Sea, made their fortunes principally by extortion, requiring passing ships to pay protection money. This allowed for a considerable economy of forces on the part of the *kaizoku*, who confined themselves to attacking only those ships whose captains had been unwise enough not to pay up. The people of the shores of neighbouring provinces paid them tribute each year, for fear of being destroyed if they refused. Their 'toll barriers of the sea' were very effective, and totally undiscriminating in respect of whom they challenged.

⚓ In this painting Chinese soldiers fight a group of marauding Japanese pirates. The pirate gangs who raided in China and Korea were known as *wako*, a two-character expression in which the first syllable indicates the country of Japan, though *wako* gangs often included Chinese and Korean sailors.

Last, but by no means least, I am sure you have heard of the Spanish Main (see p. 21). It is the most romantic place of all in connection with piracy. The word 'main' comes from 'mainland', and refers to the Spanish Empire's territories in the New World of America. Following Christopher Columbus's famous voyage of exploration to the Americas in 1492, the Spanish began to exploit the area's vast wealth in gold and silver. Silver was brought to the ports by mule train, and goods from the Far East were brought across the Pacific and taken overland to the Atlantic Ocean for reloading onto ships bound for Spain. English privateers started to raid these great treasure fleets, creating havoc, until about fifty years ago, when the Spanish authorities clamped down. The busiest places on the Spanish Main include Cartagena in Colombia and Portobello in Panama. Captain Henry Morgan captured Panama City in spectacular fashion in 1668, and it took his men – a small pirate army – fourteen days to loot it.

←«« The prime targets for the buccaneers of the Caribbean were the great Spanish treasure ships conveying gold and silver to Spain. In this picture from the *Harmsworth History of the World*, small boats containing buccaneers approach the stern of a massive Spanish galleon.

⚑ Map of the Spanish Main during the Golden Age of Piracy. The European settlements and naval trade routes in this gold-rich region were a great lure for marauding pirates, and the craggy coastlines of the many islands littering the Gulf provided ideal hideouts for pirate bands between raids.

Henry Morgan lived during what we call 'the Golden Age of Piracy', which lasted from about 1650 to 1730. Many of the scoundrels you will read about in these pages were active during this glorious era, which ended about fifty years ago when the Spanish Empire's power declined. Britain and France took over the Spanish Main and began to stamp out piracy in those waters. Both navies ruthlessly hunted down pirates throughout the Caribbean, dispensing quick and summary justice to anyone they caught, so most pirates moved elsewhere. Many famous pirates, such as Stede Bonnet, shifted their operations north to the coasts of New England, where they could target booming trade ports. Black Bart gave up on the New World altogether and moved to Africa. But have we seen the last of the pirates? We have not! Read on!

Pirates today and where to find them

Now that you know something of the history of piracy, let's take a more detailed look at where pirates are still to be found in this year of 1793.

THE ENGLISH CHANNEL

Privateers and fierce corsairs still operate across the Channel separating England and France. English sailors refer to the French's main base, St Malo, as the 'wasps' nest'. This fortified town on the coast of Brittany was once so notorious that in 1693 the English attempted to blow it up from the relative safety of the sea, sending in a 'fireship' – a vessel that was towed into a port and deliberately set alight. This 'infernal machine', as its makers called it, used the latest technology to transform an old hulk into a floating bomb, packed with barrels of gunpowder and other incendiary devices, and with old cannons strewn across its decks that would serve as shrapnel when the ship exploded. Unfortunately for the English, as it was being set in place the ship struck a rock, and the sea water that rushed into the breach dampened the gunpowder. When they lit the fuse only a very small explosion occurred; the sole casualty was a cat. The corsairs simply laughed and, humiliated, the English abandoned their offensive. The pirate trade from St Malo has passed from father to son and is now so profitable that it even attracts sponsors for privateering.

MALTA

Malta is a little island off the southern coast of Sicily that houses a bunch of corsairs who

↑ New incendiary technology transformed old vessels into explosive weapons of war.

Map of the Mediterranean during the Golden Age of Piracy.

think themselves very important indeed. They call themselves the Knights of St John, an extremely grand title for a pirate, because they are descended from Crusaders who set up hospitals in the Holy Land. They had several homes after that, including the Greek island of Rhodes, but they are now ensconced on Malta and regard themselves as the defenders of Christianity against Islam. They still regularly clash with the Barbary corsairs. As a strategic base, Malta has much to recommend it. The Order of St John converted the rocky island into a formidable galley port where Spanish fleets can rest and re-arm. It is an amazing sight today, and the Maltese ships that operate from it are formidable vessels. They have good sail power in addition to oars.

THE BALEARIC ISLANDS

The main Balearic islands are Majorca, Menorca and Ibiza. They lie in the western Mediterranean, east of Spain and north of the Barbary Coast. They have attracted pirate activity for hundreds of years. Aroudj

⚓ Battle of Port Mahon, Menorca. In May of 1756 a French task force under the Duc de Richelieu attacked the harbour of Port Mahon on Menorca, then a pillar of British naval power in the Mediterranean.

Barbarossa, one of the most legendary of the Barbary corsairs, launched an attack on Menorca in 1535; the walls you see today around Port Mahon were built by the islanders as a response to the Islamic threat. Privateers have continued to flock to the islands ever since. Take for example Jaime Scarmichi Guivernau, who commanded a privateer ship of twenty-four guns in 1778 before giving up his pirate career for the Portuguese navy. In 1784, he was involved in a privateer attack on Algiers. By contrast, his contemporary, the former privateer Francisco Catala Sitges, did not raid elsewhere but stayed on Menorca and protected local shipping from pirates. Yes, there is much activity still to be seen around these islands.

NORTH AMERICA

This is one part of the world where civilians draw a firm distinction between pirates and privateers. Very famous pirates like Blackbeard operated off the coast of North America, but no American will ever brag about Blackbeard's adventures – he was an English pirate, and thus regarded as a criminal. Instead, you will hear stories of how brave their own American privateers were when they rose up against the British during the recent American Revolution, and even the most staunch monarchist must admit that the figures are most impressive. The rebels initially possessed a navy of only thirty-four ships, and so called on about 400 privateers, who thus became crucial in the struggle for independence – they captured 3,000 British vessels during the Revolution, crippling British commerce and seizing much-needed muskets and gunpowder for the Continental Army. Many American privateers sailed from Philadelphia, the largest colonial port of the day, or from Baltimore, where shipbuilders converted merchant ships to meet the needs of the privateers. There was never a shortage of volunteers hoping to bag a share of the action by joining a privateer's crew – the men who served sailed under the rule of 'no prey, no pay', only receiving shares of any plunder. Some returned home wealthy men; the most successful privateer, a brig called *Yankee* out of Bristol, Rhode Island, captured forty prizes worth millions.

THE INDIAN OCEAN

When the Spanish Main became too dangerous for pirates, hounded by the navies as they were, many of them turned their attentions to the Indian Ocean, there being much opportunity for the patient pirate in these waters. Rich Muslims from the East make pilgrimages to Mecca along these routes, while Britain's East India Company and its Dutch equivalent send merchantmen to conduct trade with the Far East. Those ships have to

↥ The crest of Great Britain's East India Company. Their ships were tempting targets for pirates.

round the Cape of Good Hope, where they are faced by the island of Madagascar, once an ideal pirate base. The East Indiamen carry silk, fine china and precious metals, just like the old treasure fleets of the Spanish Main, and pirate raids on these ships have been among the most lucrative in history. The first pirate captain to acquire notoriety in the Indian Ocean was Henry Avery, who in 1695 headed a small pirate fleet that captured the *Ganj-i-Sawai* (or *Gunsway*), a treasure ship belonging to India's Mughal Emperor. Following a bloody fight, Avery and his gang made off with a huge amount of loot. This aroused the ire of the Emperor, and soon the pirates' paradise island of Madagascar had to be fortified. In the 1690s, St. Mary's on Madagascar boasted a population of around 1,500, and served as a vital supply base for pirates, the formidable Captain Kidd among them.

Kanhoji Angria, part of – and eventually head of – India's Maratha navy in the early eighteenth century, was active in the waters around India against the British, Dutch and Portuguese navies, earning himself the title 'pirate' among sailors of those nations, though today he is celebrated in India as a national hero. The Maratha Empire rivalled that of the Mughals; when the Maratha regime was weak, Angria exercised greater independence, attacking British ships belonging to the East India Company. His superiors sent an army against him in 1713 to curb his desire for independence, but he defeated them. After the ensuing negotiations, he became the commander of a local fleet. In spite of negotiated treaties, which he sometimes initiated, he continually harassed English and Portuguese merchant ships over a period of twenty-five years and eventually controlled almost the entire west coast of India.

THE FAR EAST

Most of the fearsome *wako* and *kaizoku* who once terrorized land and sea alike in the Far East have now been eliminated thanks to the Royal Navy and the warships of the East India Company, but some pirates do persist in the area. The marauders now primarily come from China rather than Japan, because the Japanese government forbids ships to leave Japan.

🏹 *Wako* pirates preparing to go raiding ashore on their canoes in Ming dynasty (16th-century) China or Korea, brandishing their bows and arrows and *katanas*, a typical form of Japanese long sword.

They prey mainly upon international shipping. Until quite recently, Dutch pirates were also active off Japan, from their base on the island of Hirado, raiding Portuguese vessels on their journeys between Macao and Nagasaki.

How do I become a pirate?

Well, if you've got this far, your mind must be set on being a pirate. So how do you become one? The choice may not be entirely your own; many people turn to piracy out of sheer desperation. During the Golden Age of Piracy, about twenty-five to thirty per cent of pirates were 'cimarrons' – African slaves who had escaped from their Spanish masters. Other men cruelly destined for a life of slavery joined crews after pirates had attacked the ships on which they were being transported to the New World. Bartholomew Roberts had 88 black pirates among

SAMUEL BELLAMY.

Wreck of the Whydaw

⬆ A c. 1888 lithograph showing a mournful Samuel Bellamy before his sinking ship.

his crew of 368 in 1721, and when Sam Bellamy and his fellow pirates seized the *Whydah Gally*, 25 liberated slaves joined his crew. Another former slave, Peter Cloise, became a pirate after Edward Davis took him from his 'owner' in 1679. They became close companions and went on pirating expeditions in the Caribbean and along the Pacific coast of South America.

Similarly, Diego Grillo, also known as El Mulato due to his mixed African and Spanish ancestry, escaped from Havana, Cuba, and took to the sea, joining Henry Morgan's famous sack of Panama in 1671, in which he captained a ship mounting ten guns. He and his crew made a living by attacking Spanish ships throughout the Caribbean and selling the booty in Tortuga, a notorious pirate haven. Three ships were sent to capture him, but he defeated them all and slaughtered every sailor aboard who had been born in Spain. He was eventually captured in 1673 and hanged – an unusual fate, because after capture black pirates were often treated very differently by the authorities from their white comrades (for whom hanging was not exceptional at all), often being returned to the men who 'owned' them, or sold into slavery under someone else. On board, however, no one takes the slightest notice of any man's origins or the colour of his skin. They are all part of a brotherhood of the sea.

The desperate urge to turn to piracy may also be brought about by poverty and unemployment. When a nation goes to war, it eagerly recruits lots of men to serve in its navy, but when peace comes, those same men (or at least the survivors among them) are forced to find other employment or die of starvation; those who know only the trade of sailing may have no alternative but to join a pirate crew. In the years following the War of the Spanish Succession, which lasted from 1701 to 1715, there was a particularly strong upsurge in piracy, no doubt influenced by the English Royal Navy's dismissal of 40,000 of the 53,000 men it had employed in the combat. Ironically, many of these men were almost certainly press-ganged into the navy in the first place. The Impress Service, or press gang, was an officially sanctioned way in which drunken men were literally taken from the streets of port towns and forced to become sailors.

⚓ Detail from an 18th-century painting by Peter Monamy showing the Quay at Bristol. Many a drunken wanderer of this dock was plucked from the street and forced into the service of the Royal Navy. By contrast, most pirates were volunteers.

Pirates don't use press gangs; we simply apply our 'persuasive methods' to captured crews to convince them to join our ranks. Men who have

The bravest pirate captains were often the most ruthless and could be very cruel when the situation demanded. Here Henry Morgan is apparently torturing prisoners, the crew of a captured ship. Are they being forced to reveal where they have hidden their treasure?

withstood these techniques have been known to be marooned. Four young members of the pirate George Cusack's crew are known to have been serving either as cabin boys or as apprentices to other crewmen, such as the carpenter or a musician, on the merchant ships from which they were plucked. Being of an impressionable age and living among the adult pirates, they may have more readily adapted to this wayward life than forced men and even, in time, adopted the pirates' values while learning the trade of plundering and seamanship.

So if you sail on a merchantman but secretly long for the pirate life, perhaps you will get lucky and be captured by a dastardly gang. The young John King, a nine-year-old passenger of the *Bonetta*, surprised everyone – not least his own mother – when he asked to join Black Sam Bellamy's pirate crew after they had taken the ship. According to the official testimony of the master of the *Bonetta*, such was King's determination to join the pirates' ranks that he declared he would throw himself overboard if they did not take him on, and even threatened his mother with violence when she attempted to stop him. He was successful in his bid to become a pirate, but sadly his career was to last only three short months; he lost his life when Bellamy's ship, the *Whydah*, was wrecked, along with all but two of the crew.

Perhaps piracy is in your blood; captains have been known to take their own sons along on raids, to teach them the trade. During a battle with a Dutch ship, the French corsair Jean Bart noticed that his fourteen-year-old son was flinching at the sound of gunfire. He tied the lad to the mast so that he would get used to 'this kind of music', as he put it. But child pirates are the exception, not the norm; Black Bart's Pirates Code (see p. 146) clearly stated that 'No prudent Woman, or Boy, is to be brought aboard', referring specifically to children (and also to women, though this did not stop some particularly driven women from pursuing the pirate life).

The reluctant pirate's guide to alternative maritime careers

Are you terribly disappointed? Have you set your heart on a seafaring career, but can't face the prospect of being hanged? There are alternatives, you know. Have you considered becoming a pilot? They guide ships out of port on to the open sea; it's a less stimulating occupation, but perhaps if you mumble you can maintain a reputation as a pirate. Otherwise, if your mind is dead set on going to sea, why not join a merchantman's crew? This is a great way to see a pirate battle in action. Unfortunately, you are likely to be the focus of that action, but it will certainly be very exciting if you survive. Or perhaps you might join the Royal Navy, though conditions on board His Majesty's ships are so bad that their sailors often long for the life of a pirate.

If you fancy living outside the law, but are accustomed to the comforts of home, you may find smuggling an appealing alternative to piracy. You will convey contraband goods from ships lying offshore to secret hiding places on the coast. The money is good, and you might get to meet real pirates. You may even indulge in a little trickery, causing ships to wreck themselves on

>>→ Two grim-faced smugglers await the ships that bear their illicit wares. Their weary, listless expressions promise none of the excitement that the life of a pirate offers.

your coastline. Try it on a dark and stormy night. Place a lantern near some rocks to fool a ship's captain into thinking he is heading for a safe harbour. When the ship crashes into the rocks and starts to sink, the cargo will be yours for the taking, and then you can go home to the comfort of your own (dry) bed.

In my own fair land, smuggling was once quite easy; most smugglers were fishermen by trade, and considered too poor to pay fines, so interference from revenue agents was rare. Most were also too old to be impressed into the Royal Navy. But everything changed in 1736, when Parliament enacted the Smugglers Act. Now smugglers are arrested and punished, and if a revenue man is wounded, the court is entitled to impose the death penalty. Even smugglers who don't use weapons may be transported to a distant land, sentenced to hard labour, whipped, or – worst of all – pressed into the Royal Navy. Might as well be a pirate after all...

2

Role Models

Pirates are a varied stock – men and women from all over the world have been drawn to the opportunity to make a living by tricking or intimidating more honest sailors out of their wealth, and there is much to be learned by studying their careers. Will you model your captaincy on the clever Blackbeard, who carefully cultivated rumours of his terrible deeds so as to spark fear into the hearts of his prey before even laying his hand on a cutlass, or the brutal William Kidd, whose remorseless savagery outshone any fabricated tale? Will you charge recklessly into battle, like the brave – some might say foolish – John Paul Jones, or use trickery to gain the upper hand over your unsuspecting victims, like the cunning Rachel Wall?

Some of the most famous marauders were called pirates by everyone they encountered; for others, there is a certain sensitivity about the title. You will certainly be regarded as a villain by your victims, but you may find yourself celebrated at home as a great hero. Which draws your imagination – the respect and dread that you will inspire through global infamy, or the glory of your fellow countrymen's admiration?

Read through these careers very carefully, and decide for yourself if this is the way you really want to live (or die).

The Barbarossa brothers
(active around 1512–1546)

ORUSCE en HAREADEN BARBAROSSA
Coninghen Tunis en Algiers en opper Zee rooghst

↟ A 17th-century Dutch engraving of the Barbarossa Brothers. After Aroudj died in battle, his younger brother took up the mantle and terrorized the North African coast, eventually coming to control the territory between Morocco and Djerba.

The two Barbarossa brothers, perhaps the most famous of the Barbary corsairs, were originally from the Greek island of Lesbos and operated out of La Goletta in Tunisia. The older brother, Aroudj, born around 1470, was given the name 'Barbarossa' because of his red beard. By 1512 Aroudj commanded twelve galleys and 1,000 men-at-arms, and was known far and wide for his daring exploits. In 1518, six years after losing his arm during an attack on a Spanish garrison, Aroudj died in battle. His younger brother, Kheir ed-Din, dyed his beard and hair red with henna as an homage to his dead brother, and picked up the pirate mantle, seizing several Tunisian ports and transforming them into pirate havens, in which he lived off the plunder garnered from his naval exploits. In 1529, he captured the Spanish fort at Algiers, all that was left of the former Spanish presence in the area. Finally, in 1534, he deposed the Bey (ruler) of Tunis, Muley Hassan, thereby assuring his own dominance of the coast from Morocco to Djerba, the largest North African island, off the coast of Tunisia. He spent the rest of his days fighting various Christian enemies, including a Holy League fleet specifically formed by the Pope to destroy him, passing away in 1546 from fever. While Aroudj was famous in his day, it was Kheir ed-Din who would earn the Barbarossa brothers their place in history, the tenacity he shared with his brother tempered by his own prudence to ensure a long and fruitful pirate career.

Murakami Takeyoshi (1533–1604)

↟ Murakami Yoshimitsu, the leader of the *kaizoku* pirates from the Innoshima branch of the Murakami family on Japan's Inland Sea, who specialized in extracting tolls from ships passing through the busy waters. Unlike the *wako*, *kaizoku* preyed upon their own people.

The most famous family name associated with the *kaizoku*, or 'pirate kings', of Japan's Inland Sea is Murakami. There were three active branches of this powerful family, based on the major islands Noshima, Kurushima and Innoshima – three of some 3,000 in the Inland Sea. Murakami Takeyoshi wore a helmet ornamented with his personal crest, a golden shell, and ruled from a castle on the island of Noshima overlooking one of the busiest and narrowest straits of the region. The Murakami claimed protection money at toll barriers; alternatively, sea captains could purchase a guarantee of safe passage in advance, in the form of a flag bearing the Murakami family crest. This granted them immunity from further toll charges or any piratical activity within the Murakami domains. If ships' captains refused to pay a toll, they laid themselves open to attack by the Murakami navy, who would sail up close to board their victims, hailing arrows down upon them, as well as various explosive devices. When the Murakami went into battle their customary farewell meal included octopus, a symbolic choice, its eight arms protecting it against enemies from all directions.

Zheng Chenggong (1624–1662)

You may know this fellow better as Coxinga. His father was a Chinese merchant (and pirate) based on the Japanese island of Hirado, and his mother was Japanese. At the age of seven he was taken by his family to China. There he prospered, even passing several of the imperial examinations that were required by the ruling Ming dynasty if a man was to enter high office. He continued to be a loyal supporter of the Ming dynasty when they were threatened by the Manchus, invaders from the north. Zheng Chenggong fought for the Ming first as a general on dry land, but when he

was forced to retreat to southern China he took refuge on the sea and attacked Manchu ships. The Manchus were not the only ones to feel his wrath – the Dutch colonists on the island of Taiwan became the target of a massive raid, seen by the Europeans as a pirate incursion. It culminated in a

←« Coxinga was the son of a Chinese pirate and a Japanese woman. After serving the Chinese military for a time as a general in the Ming army, he took to the sea. His raid on the Dutch Fort Zeelandia marked the end of European colonialism on Taiwan.

siege of Fort Zeelandia, a stronghold of the Dutch East India Company; Zheng secured its surrender on 1 February 1662. That was the end of Dutch rule on Taiwan, which Zheng proceeded to use as a base for raiding Manchu shipping. More accusations of piracy followed when Zheng raided the Philippines, but his plans for a major attack, and possibly even the expulsion of the Spanish from the Philippines, were foiled when malaria struck him down at the age of thirty-seven.

Stenka Razin (1630–1671)

The Cossack tribes of Russia fished in the Don River, hunted in the vast grassland plains of the steppe and herded sheep, cattle and horses, but when these resources ran dry, poverty forced some to turn to piracy in order to survive. This is how, in April 1667, Stenka Razin took to marauding on the Caspian Sea. He led a number of great assaults on trading vessels belonging to the Tsar, the ruler of Russia, appropriating their rich cargoes and releasing political prisoners, and he quickly gained a formidable reputation: when his fleet sailed past the great fortress at Tsaritsyn, the guns remained silent in acknowledgment of his invincibility. In July he arrived at a walled town on the Caspian Sea coast, which belonged to the Persian Empire at that time. By disguising himself as a pilgrim wishing to pray in the cathedral, Stenka, along with a band of forty pirates, slipped past the guards and infiltrated the town. What was initially a peaceful affair turned bloody when the garrison commander and 170 soldiers refused to

⚑ Stenka Razin, a pirate who acted like a privateer when it suited him, made many enemies among Russia's friends and foes alike. On 6 June 1671, after a series of cruel punishments, he was executed in Moscow's Red Square. This wooden bust of him is by Beatrice Sandomirskaya.

join the pirates. They were promptly killed. The pirates remained there all winter, but they were growing short of food and water. The Persians attacked them again and again, and finally the government reclaimed the city. Stenka escaped, and shortly afterwards he carried out another raid and capture two Persian treasure-ships. He was pursued by the Russian navy but, to avoid a fight, Stenka accepted a full pardon, on condition that he peacefully return to the Don River. Fearing retribution from the authorities, his fellow Cossacks captured him and handed him over for punishment. Transported to Moscow, the seat of the government's power, he was flogged and branded, and suffered a cruel and unusual ordeal as his head was shaved and subjected to a constant drip of freezing water. On 6 June 1671, Stenka Razin was executed in the Red Square by quartering.

Henry Morgan (1635–1688)

The Welsh privateer Henry Morgan operated in the Spanish Main in the Golden Age of Piracy, most famously sacking the Spanish territory of Panama. When the Spanish counter-attacked he made a human shield out of priests, women and the mayor, an act that earned him a reputation for cruelty. This was the first of many brutal land raids at his hand. When the news reached Europe, Spain was outraged, because the raid had happened while Spain and England were at peace, having signed a treaty. Henry Morgan was summoned to England in April 1672 and spent two years technically under house arrest, although in reality he was allowed to come and go as he pleased – he was very popular in England on account of having fought the Spanish. He was even consulted by the government on how to improve Jamaica's defences. Not surprisingly, he was eventually found innocent of any wrongdoing, and instead of being hanged he was knighted and sent back to Jamaica as Lieutenant Governor. Morgan is considered by many to be one of Great Britain's finest warriors, a superb

<< Portrait of Sir Henry Morgan from *The Buccaneers of America*, a chronicle of the pirate activity in Central America in the 17th century written by the Frenchman (or possibly Dutchman) Alexander Exquemelin and first published in Dutch in 1678. Morgan was a controversial figure. In England his crimes were ignored because he had committed them against the Spanish. In Spain he was loathed as a pirate guilty of grave atrocities.

military strategist with leadership qualities to boot. The Spanish argue that he committed terrible atrocities, including torture, on their people, but when he died on Jamaica in 1688 he was given a state funeral and an amnesty was granted to his fellow pirates so that they could come and pay their last respects.

William Kidd (1645–1701)

William Kidd was a Scotsman who was hired as a privateer by the governor of New York to attack ships belonging to the French – and to hunt down some of the most famous pirates of the day, including Thomas Tew. His backers were so supportive that they actually bought him a ship, the *Adventure Galley*, and fitted it out, but the ungrateful Kidd soon took matters into his own hands. In 1696, he crossed the Atlantic to West Africa, where he attacked a ship belonging to the East India Company, a number of Portuguese vessels and even a British ship, so it would appear that his attitude towards piracy had changed from chasing them to becoming one himself. He gained a reputation for indiscriminate brutality, not only torturing his prisoners but even murdering one of his own crew, hurling a metal bucket at his head and fracturing his skull. Apparently without remorse, Kidd went so far as to boast that his well-connected friends in England would ensure he faced no penalty for the crime. By the time he reached Madagascar in 1698, he had contended with a mutiny on board his own ship, and the East India Company had heard what he was up to and – not unreasonably – declared him a pirate. Captain Kidd set fire to his ship and fled. Hoping to find refuge in America, he attempted to broker a deal with the governor of Boston, who promptly had him arrested instead. Kidd was shipped back to England, where he tried the desperate defence of incriminating those who had backed him in the first place. This failed utterly, and he was found guilty of murder and piracy. He was sentenced to be hanged at Execution Dock in London on 23 May 1701. On the first attempt the rope broke, but the Sheriff's men dragged him back to the gallows, hanging him successfully the second time around. Kidd's body was painted with tar, wrapped in chains and placed in an iron cage known as a gibbet on the river bank. For almost twenty years, his body remained gibbeted as an example to other would-be pirates.

⚓ Captain William Kidd burying his Bible on the Plymouth Sound, on the English Channel, just before his final, doomed voyage. 19th-century historians thought this act sealed his fate.

Captain Kidd is one of the few pirates known to have buried his treasure. We know about this because most of it was found – so I wouldn't recommend the practice!

Réné Duguay-Trouin (1673–1736)

As a boy, the great French corsair Réné Duguay-Trouin wanted to become
a priest, but by the age of sixteen he had cast off these pious ambitions
and joined the French navy. During the first three months of his service
he boarded an English ship, endured a violent storm and almost died in
a fire on board; far more excitement than he might have experienced in
a monastery! Clearly he made an impression on his superiors, as he was

A 19th-century engraving of St
Malo, or 'the wasps' nest', as it was
known by the English. This was the
site of the failed fireship attack of
1693, just one year before Duguay-
Trouin escaped his British captors.

promoted to full command of a fourteen-gun
privateer ship when he was only eighteen. Over
the course of his naval career he captured five
more English ships before being captured by
the English authorities in 1694 and slung into
a Plymouth gaol. Somehow he escaped and made his way back to St Malo,
that great pirate stronghold on the French side of the English Channel (or
as the French know it, La Manche, 'the Sleeve'). In 1696, he and his new

ship captured some Dutch vessels, for which he was made a Commander in the French navy. Moving further afield, he captured Rio de Janeiro in 1711; quite a feat, with his twelve ships and 6,000 men pitted against defending forces of five forts and twice as many soldiers. The battle lasted eleven days, but proved worthwhile, earning his sponsors double their initial investments. Despite the great wealth his exploits earned him, he frittered it all away on a lavish lifestyle, and when he lay dying in 1736, he wrote to his king to ask for support for his family.

Blackbeard (around 1680–1718)

Edward Teach must be the most famous pirate in history, but I sometimes wonder why this should be. His career lasted only two years, and he hardly ever risked his life in open battle, preferring instead to attack lightly armed vessels. Now you may say that this is very sensible, and you'd be right, but the strange thing is that, in spite of all this commendable cunning, Blackbeard is best known for being very fierce. It was a reputation that he exploited whenever he could, and his image grew with the telling. He was supposed to be a giant of a man, and liked experimenting with his image, trying to look as intimidating as possible – he twisted ribbons into his great mane of hair, kept two swords always at his waist and even balanced smouldering matches behind his ears. He was also known, of course, for the fine black beard that gave him his nickname. Blackbeard was a menace to the seaboard of North America's Carolinas, ambushing trade and passenger vessels alike. He was a shrewd operator, and eventually moved his activity ashore; with an army of 300 pirates, he blockaded Charleston Harbour and took a number of hostages, threatening to kill them unless supplies were delivered. Though they held the city to ransom for weeks, no supplies came, but neither did Blackbeard kill the men.

It took the governor of neighbouring Virginia to stand up to him, a man named Alexander Spotswood. Because the waters where Blackbeard

↑ This picture of the death of Blackbeard illustrates the romantic light in which pirates are commonly viewed. Everyone knows the name of Blackbeard, but who can identify the name of the brave lieutenant who defeated him?

was operating were shallow, the Governor bought two small ships and sent them into action under Lieutenant Robert Maynard, who was promised a rich reward for Blackbeard's capture, dead or alive. When Maynard approached at dawn, Blackbeard drew the two sloops after him and cleverly managed to ground both in the shoals. But once freed, Maynard closed on Blackbeard, whose own ship then ran aground. Blackbeard had always tried to avoid battles, but now he had no choice but to fight. He launched a broadside at Maynard's vessel, causing a fire to break out on the deck. Blackbeard's men boarded recklessly, as they could see very few survivors through the smoke, but as the pirates swarmed onto the ship they were subjected to a furious counter-attack by the crew, who had taken cover below decks, that took them by surprise. Most of the boarding party surrendered, but Blackbeard fought on. He discharged his pistol at Maynard. The shot missed, and Maynard's return fire wounded him. Despite his injury, Blackbeard struck down with his cutlass with enough force to break Maynard's sword. Maynard appeared to be helpless, but as Blackbeard moved in for the kill one of the sailors slashed him in the neck. Blackbeard fought on even though he was losing much blood, and more strength. Eye-witnesses later reported that it took a total of twenty-five shots and cuts to finish him off. Blackbeard's head was cut off and hung from the bowsprit, so that Maynard's paymaster could see that he had earned his reward.

Bartholomew Roberts (1682–1722)

Known for his flair for fashion, typically sporting a diamond cross and a red feather in his hat, Black Bart was the archetypal pirate captain, with a natural nose for treasure. In fact, he captured more ships than any other pirate of his day. Roberts changed his given name, John, upon joining a pirate ship in order to confuse the authorities, hoping to avoid arrest, and indeed his pirate career got off to a good start. After selling the loot he gained from assaulting a Portuguese convoy in New England, he went on pirate cruises off Newfoundland in a fine new vessel he had traded for the Portuguese ships themselves. He named his new ship *Royal Fortune*, and fortune certainly favoured him; he netted prizes of fifteen French or English ships and one Dutch vessel within the space of four days in the Caribbean. He continued in this lively vein until 1722, when he was approached by a naval frigate – a well-built, well-equipped warship – the

⚓ Bartholomew Roberts proudly stands before his ship, along with captured merchantmen, in the background. Copper engraving from Captain Charles Johnson's *A General History of the Robberies and Murders of the most notorious Pyrates*.

HMS *Swallow*. Black Bart, confident on the back of his previous victories, steered towards it with a boarding party prepared, but a hail of grapeshot caught him in the throat, killing him instantly. It seems his luck had finally run out.

Stede Bonnet
(1688–1718)

Here was a fine fellow indeed! Captain Johnson's excellent book, *A General History of the Robberies and Murders of the most notorious Pyrates*, tells

A GENERAL

HISTORY

OF THE

Robberies and Murders

Of the moſt notorious

PYRATES,

AND ALSO

Their *Policies*, *Diſcipline* and *Goverament*,

From their firſt RISE and SETTLEMENT in the Iſland of *Providence*, in 1717, to the preſent Year 1724.

WITH

The remarkable ACTIONS and ADVENTURES of the two Female Pyrates, *Mary Read* and *Anne Bonny*.

To which is prefix'd

An ACCOUNT of the famous Captain *Avery* and his Companions; with the Manner of his Death in *England*.

The Whole digeſted into the following CHAPTERS;

Chap. I. Of Captain *Avery*.	VIII. Of Captain *England*.
II. The Riſe of Pyrates.	IX. Of Captain *Davis*.
III. Of Captain *Martel*.	X. Of Captain *Roberts*.
IV. Of Captain *Bonnet*.	XI. Of Captain *Worley*.
V. Of Captain *Thatch*.	XII. Of Captain *Lowther*.
VI. Of Captain *Vane*.	XIII. Of Captain *Low*.
VII. Of Captain *Rackam*.	XIV. Of Captain *Evans*.

And theſe ſeveral Crews.

To which is added,

A ſhort ABSTRACT of the Statute and Civil Law, in Relation to PYRACY.

By Captain CHARLES JOHNSON.

LONDON, Printed for *Ch. Rivington* at the *Bible* and *Crown* in St. *Paul's-Church-Yard*, *J. Lacy* at the *Ship* near the *Temple-Gate*, and *J. Stone* next the *Crown* Coffee-houſe the back of *Greys-Inn*, 1724.

us that Stede Bonnet once owned a plantation on Barbados, and was even a major in the island's militia. Unfortunately no one can prove this – we pirates, being creative types, have a tendency to 'embellish' our achievements, and I am sure you will be no different. Stede Bonnet was very active off the Carolinas in 1718. He was injured in a battle with the Spanish and soon after encountered Blackbeard, to whom he voluntarily surrendered control of his ship. He and Blackbeard sailed together for a time, but Bonnet's own crew preferred Blackbeard's command, and he became disillusioned with the pirate life. When he heard that Britain was at war with Spain, giving him the chance to become a legal privateer, he jumped at the opportunity. He was granted a pardon for his previous piratical endeavours, and dutifully preyed on Spanish shipping, but eventually grew greedy once again. The authorities in Charleston placed a £700 bounty on his head, and

≪≪ The title page of Captain Charles Johnson's *A General History of the Robberies and Murders of the most notorious Pyrates*, first published *c.* 1724 to instant commercial success.

≫≫ The public hanging of Stede Bonnet, along with the rest of his crew, in Charleston in 1718. Whatever romantic notions we may entertain about the pirate's life, this is how many pirates meet their death.

found him and his shipmates on Sullivan's Island, near the entrance of the harbour. Bonnet abandoned his lair and fled upriver with a few companions, but his determined pursuers tracked him down and a five-hour-long battle ensued. Bonnet surrendered after everyone else in his party was shot dead. He was tried in Charleston, found guilty despite mounting his own impassioned defence, and hanged along with the rest of his crew.

Samuel Bellamy (1689–1717)

I am sure you have heard many tales about Black Sam, as everyone called him in Cape Cod. This nickname came from his habit of tying his long hair back using a simple black band – a sensible alternative to the powdered wig that was so fashionable, but most inconvenient on board ship. Otherwise he dressed very finely, and always liked to carry four pistols and a sword. He was a clever tactician, sometimes sending out decoy ships to confuse an enemy vessel so that his own strike came as a surprise. Yet he was also known for his generous and merciful spirit; he never murdered captives, and instead was so kind that many of them joined his crew, earning him the additional nickname 'The Prince of Pirates'.

Black Sam was born in Devon, a part of England that has produced many great seafaring men. As a young man he signed up with the Royal Navy, and fought in several battles before emigrating to the American colonies in 1715 and settling in Cape Cod, now part of the state of Massachusetts. He didn't stay there for long – hearing that there was vast wealth to be obtained off the coast of Florida, where a Spanish treasure fleet had recently been wrecked, he set off southwards to find it. This salvage scheme turned out to be a bust, so Black Sam decided to change tack: the treasure hunter became a pirate. He and his companions joined the crew of Captain Benjamin Hornigold on the ship *Marianne* (where the first mate just happened to be a certain Edward Teach, soon to gain great notoriety as Blackbeard).

Bellamy had aspirations of his own, and his opportunity to rise to greatness came when the *Marianne*'s crew, frustrated by Hornigold's reluctance to attack ships from his homeland, England, mounted a mutiny. Bellamy won the vote for Hornigold's replacement, and so became Captain Black Sam. He was a wise and fair captain, governing his crew according to a democratically conceived set of rules; he believed that piracy simply offered men born to the lower classes a chance to escape the vicious cycle of poverty that was all they could otherwise hope for. He did not disappoint his crew, leading successful raids on fifty ships within his first year at the helm.

In 1717, Black Sam captured the magnificent *Whydah Gally*, a slave ship that was on the return leg of its maiden voyage, carrying the fortune earned from the sale of slaves. Bellamy chased it for three days in the straits between Cuba and Hispaniola before getting near enough to fire a single shot – but that was enough. The captain lowered his flag in surrender. Typically magnanimous in victory, Bellamy exchanged one of his own

⚓ The excitement of a boarding operation is captured in this painting of the boarding of the *Whydah Gally* by Black Sam Bellamy's crew: both sides are brandishing pistols and cutlasses as the pirates clamber up the rigging, while in the background, Black Sam Bellamy's remaining crew on the flagship prepare another small boat to bring reinforcements to join in the fight.

vessels for the *Whydah Gally*, and proceeded to refit his prize as a pirate ship.

With this vessel, now simply called the *Whydah*, under his command, Black Sam sailed north for the seas off the coast of New England. Continuing his winning streak, on 26 April 1717 he captured the *Mary Anne*, which had a hold full of Madeira wine. He placed some of his crew on board and set off again on his course, but there was disaster ahead. Bellamy's fleet became separated in dense fog, and the *Whydah* met with a violent storm off Cape Cod. It was driven bow-first onto a sandbar by the hurricane-force winds, where the masts broke under the pounding of forty-foot-high waves, and the ship sank quickly, taking Black Sam and all but two of his crew with her, swept over the side by the raging surf. The *Mary Anne* was wrecked the same night. The few survivors of the two ships were tried for piracy in Boston, and six of them were hanged. It was a sad end to Bellamy's glorious pirate career.

Anne Bonny (1700–1782)

Anne Bonny, the illegitimate daughter of an Irish lawyer, travelled to the New World as a young girl with her parents, her father having divorced his wife and consequently faced persecution and a loss of business in London. When she was only a teenager, Anne's mother died of typhoid, and her relationship with her father deteriorated when she fell in love with and married a poor sailor named James Bonny. The pair moved to Nassau, an island in the Bahamas renowned as a pirate haven, but surrounded by such daring souls she quickly grew disillusioned with her husband's lack of valour. She turned to the company of many different men, among whom was 'Calico Jack' Rackham, captain of a pirate ship. She abandoned her husband and joined Rackham's crew. They knew she was a woman, but she dressed and acted like a man, drinking and fighting profusely, and her victims thought she was male. The infamous Mary Read joined their crew in 1720. A formidable pirate herself, she coaxed the crew on to even greater bloodshed and violence. However, in November of the same year they were all captured by the Royal Navy and sentenced to death. Both Anne Bonny and Mary Read claimed clemency for pregnancy in prison, and their death sentences weren't carried out (though Mary died in prison). No one is sure how the famous female pirate died, though there is speculation that she returned home to her husband or her father and lived out the rest of her days peacefully.

⚓ Anne Bonny was one of the few women certainly known to have joined the crews of marauding buccaneers.

John Paul Jones (1747–1792)

'Surrender? I have not yet begun to fight!' Those were the stirring words uttered during battle by one of the finest privateers of all time. His name was John Paul Jones and he was born in Scotland. He sailed for Virginia in 1760, and there became deeply involved in the American revolutionary cause. As a lieutenant in the American navy he was ordered to Brest, northern France, in 1775, from where he could prey on British

⚓ Captain John Paul Jones in the midst of battle, smoking pistol in one hand and sword in the other. This courageous privateer is celebrated in the United States of America as the father of their navy.

ships. Within three years he was also carrying out raids ashore, including on his homeland, Scotland. In one of his most daring exploits he planned to kidnap the Earl of Selkirk from his home in Kirkcudbright. His plans seemed scuppered when it transpired that the Earl was not at home, but undeterred from his dastardly intentions, Jones stole his silver instead, and on his way back to Brest he seized a British ship. On 1 September 1776 he was in action in American waters, off Delaware, in the sloop *Providence*, after he had captured a British whaler. A twenty-eight-gun frigate, *Solebay*, spotted him and gave chase, but Jones managed to outrun his slower pursuer, even firing a swivel gun across its bows as he escaped. New privateering commissions followed in a new ship, which he renamed *Bonhomme Richard*; originally a merchantman, the vessel had been converted to a man-of-war to support the French navy, and so was a mighty ship for any pirate to aspire to! In 1779, Jones entered the North

🔱 The *Bonhomme Richard*, before she succumbed to the sea, damaged beyond repair, after John Paul Jones' fierce fight with the British navy.

Sea with a mind to raid Leith, Scotland, but this expedition had to be cut short because of bad weather. Heading south on 3 September, he encountered a British convoy off Flamborough Head, and a tense stand-off between *Bonhomme Richard* and the lead British ship, *Serapis*, began. Neither side yielded to negotiations – instead, the ships let fly their close-quarter broadsides, and under the cover of intense musket fire, Jones boarded the *Serapis*. A fierce fight ensued. It was during this engagement that Jones uttered his famous proclamation, which ultimately proved true; far from accepting defeat, he captured the fine British vessel, though his own *Bonhomme Richard* suffered fatally from the combat, sinking despite the crew's best efforts to save her. Regardless, this was celebrated as a great victory, and John Paul Jones is greatly honoured in the country that we now call the United States of America, where he is regarded as the father of the US navy. Yet he always sought adventure, and his last commission was in the Russian navy under Empress Catherine II. He died aged forty-five in Paris in 1792.

Rachel Wall (1760–1789)

The sea had always called to Rachel, who left her family's New England farm at the age of sixteen to move to the coast. There she met her husband, a fisherman named George Wall, and for a while she worked in Boston as a maid while he was away at sea, but soon the pair were drawn to a more exciting occupation. Together with a gang of like-minded sailors, they stole a vessel, and proceeded to prey on the honest merchant ships that passed. Their cunning ploy was for Rachel to stand at the mast of an apparently wrecked ship, crying for help after a bout of rough weather. When someone came to her aid, she and her accomplices would rob them. They managed to defraud twelve crews in this manner, but in 1782 their scheme backfired when their ship actually sank in a hurricane; all were drowned except Rachel. Following her (actual) rescue, she returned to Boston and resumed working as a maid, but it was not long before she turned again to a life of crime, stealing from ships moored in Boston Harbour. Her fate was sealed when she was caught aboard a ship on which a sailor was found dead and accused of his murder. At her trial on 8 October 1789 she confessed to being a pirate, but swore that she was innocent of murder. She was the last woman to be hanged in Massachusetts, and the only known woman pirate of New England.

So there you have it. Pirates, buccaneers and privateers are a very mixed bunch. They show bravery, cunning and sometimes great cruelty. The men and women you have just read about may not be the great romantic figures you had in mind, so remember, if you become a pirate you will be judged against the example they set as you make your own way in the world. So think very carefully about how your name might one day appear in a list like this one.

3
Life on Board

Do you still have the romantic idea that pirates do nothing other than attack ships and have adventures? Well, if you think like that you will be bitterly disappointed; though the life of a pirate is undeniably one of uncertainty and danger, such excitement will occupy only a very small part of the time you spend at sea. Most of your days will be spent performing the menial duties that are yours by virtue of where you fit into the ship's company and, believe me, you will start at the bottom of the ladder – literally.

⚓

Where do you fit in?

On board ship you will be part of a hierarchy. The captain is at the top, of course, and it may surprise you to hear that captains usually become captains because they have been elected by the crew – remember Black Sam, who won his crew's favour with his fair temperament and natural sense of justice. In choosing a captain, pirates look for the one among them who can best lead by example. He must be knowledgeable, bold and 'pistol-proof'! Popularity plays only a small role in the election.

PAGE 55 Illustration of the pirate captain Robertson Keitt by Howard Pyle, 1907. Pyle shows the captain standing firmly on the swaying deck in his red coat and long sash; it is largely because of Pyle's works that such stereotypes of pirate dress gained popularity.

More crucial is that a captain commands his crew's respect; he must demonstrate bravery and cunning, be capable of handling the crew and navigating the ship, and know how to fight. Bartholomew Sharpe, for example, was a skilful navigator while being a man of undaunted courage and excellent conduct.

Second to the captain is the quartermaster. Like the captain, the quartermaster is elected to the position, which is akin to that of a sheriff, maintaining the peace on board. As the most trusted member of the crew, he mediates arguments between pirates, selects members of the boarding party before battle, oversees captured booty, keeps the ship's accounts and disburses each crewman's share of the treasure after a successful raid. Since he has to keep track of the booty and work out who is owed what, at the very least he needs to know how to count and write. 'Calico Jack' Rackham was a quartermaster before he became a pirate captain, and the role would certainly give you good training in handling your crew before moving on to captaincy.

Also essential to the crew are the first and second mates, to whom the captain delegates some of his day-to-day responsibilities, including discipline. The sailing master oversees the practical navigation and the setting of sails, with the help of the helmsman, who actually steers the ship. The boatswain (or bosun) maintains the ship, supervises the crew's day-to-day work and oversees the distribution of food and drink. The master gunner is essential aboard any pirate ship. He trains the pirates who work the guns, controls the supply of powder and shot, and commands the gun crews during battle, ensuring the ship's artillery is used to the best effect when capturing prizes and warding off attacks.

An armourer is a very useful individual to have on board. These skilled gunsmiths will keep your weapons in order and repair them when necessary. Every gun is unique, and if a part is lost, it is not easy to find a replacement. (You, of course, are responsible for keeping your own pistol clean and well-maintained and will be punished if you neglect this duty.) Wooden ships require

⚓ Cross-section view of a late 18th-century warship. Your sloop may not be as spacious, but certainly you'll have to learn to navigate the main elements shown here – armouries, living quarters, storage compartments for cargo and livestock and, of course, the dreaded bilge.

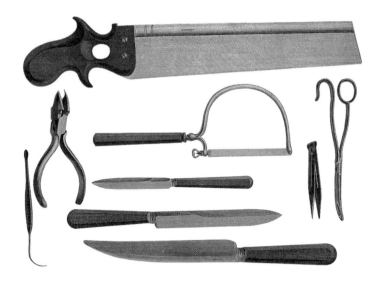

⚕ A typical 18th-century surgeon's kit. Thus equipped, your ship's doctor would be well prepared to perform an amputation if necessary – though a strong-stomached carpenter given a wide, sharp blade could do the job at a pinch.

constant maintenance, so carpenters are also very handy to have around; as well as making essential repairs, they will build furniture and masts. You should always keep an eye out for a skilled carpenter when capturing enemy ships – you will want to compel them to join your ranks.

If you are fortunate enough to capture a ship with a good surgeon on board, then immediately add them to the pirate roster, whether or not they are willing. Don't feel guilty – if the authorities catch up with you, any surgeons will be freed, as it will naturally be assumed that they were forced into the role. When a pirate ship lacks a surgeon, the carpenter usually fulfils those duties – because the two use similar tools! Another important crew member is the cook, although judging by most of the food I have tasted he is unlikely to be a skilled chef. Often, he is just an older member of the crew, or one with a disability that makes the more physically demanding work on board difficult or impossible – perhaps he lost a limb to the carpenter...

As for you – you will start out as a younker. You will notice that the word sounds a bit like 'younger', which should give you a hint as to your status. You will be one of the youngest of the foremast men, so-called because your bunks are located before (i.e. in front of) the main mast of the ship. Your superiors, by contrast, will be berthed abaft (behind) the mast. You will need to be fit and energetic, because you will be ordered to go aloft, up the mast and into the rigging, to set and furl the sails and sling the yards (which means making the ropes safe). I hope you have a head for heights. The older seamen will help hoist the sails from on deck, pulling on the ropes in coordination with your monkey-like efforts, high above their heads. As a ship depends on its sails being handled correctly – it is very unlikely you will be on an oared vessel – you will be kept very busy. This is a good thing; idleness is the enemy of good seamanship. Even when you are not dangling from the mast, you will be scrubbing the decks or scraping them clean. You could also be weighing (raising) the anchor or lowering it, wetting the ship's planking so that the caulking that seals the joins does not dry out in hot weather (letting water in), or performing any of a dozen other tasks.

You will also be required to take your turn at keeping watch, either in the team called the 'larboard (left side) watch', under the ship's quartermaster, or the 'starboard (right side) watch', under the first mate. The day at sea is divided into time periods that are four hours long and run from noon of one day to noon of the next, although the period between 4 p.m. and 8 p.m. is broken into two 'dog watches', so that no sailor has to do the same duty every single day. When you are on duty, one of your fellow pirates will have the chance to sleep, and will sling their hammock where yours is at other times; in this way, the vast machine that is served by the crew's labours can continue without a break.

Do not regard these duties as mere drudgery. You will pick up some very useful specialist skills that will stand you in good stead when you earn a higher rank, but it has, indeed, to be earned. Some skills must be learned through long observation and experience, such as steering a ship or gunnery. Navigation, a vital skill that is not shared by all, will involve many hours of study, but proficiency at navigation will be well worth all the effort you put into it. Basic navigation involves the use of landmarks, such as recognizing the shapes of islands. Aside from an acquaintance with landmarks, a navigator has to understand weather patterns. The regular rains and winds called monsoons, for example, influence the direction and times when ships travel to and from the East Indies. And the Spanish treasure fleet schedules in the Americas are (theoretically) timed to minimize the danger of hurricanes from midsummer into autumn. Observing such patterns helps pirates to plan their attacks most effectively.

A USEFUL GLOSSARY OF PIRATE EXPRESSIONS

You may not be a younker just yet, but it is never too soon to learn how to talk like a pirate. You'll become very familiar with the following non-technical expressions during your pirate career, and they may prove useful at any prospective interview with a pirate captain.

Ahoy! = Good afternoon, old chap!

Aye, aye, sir! = I will do it immediately!

Avast behind! = I say, old chap, look at that!

Arr!* = Totally meaningless; may be inserted into any conversation at will.

*NOT TO BE CONFUSED WITH 'AARGH!', AN EXPRESSION GENERALLY RESERVED FOR INCIDENTS OF EXTREME UNPLEASANTNESS.

Yo, ho, ho! = I'm feeling rather chipper today!

Splice the mainbrace! = Drink, anyone?

Batten down the hatches! = The weather looks particularly inclement.

Shiver me timbers! = I am experiencing serious and unexpected dread over the present situation.

Smartly, lad / lass! = I say, do hurry up!

Pieces of Eight! = A reference to a common form of currency, an expression normally confined to parrots.

What the well-dressed pirate is wearing

We now turn to the important matter of what is appropriate to wear on board, and the answer is not as obvious as you might think. How about a long flowing red sash, I hear you ask, and a Spanish bandana? I think you have been reading too many stories about pirates. Black Bart was a dandy among pirates; men often speak of how gorgeously he dressed, envious of his crimson waistcoat, the red feather in his hat, and the two pistols he wore slung on a sash. However, Black Bart was an exception, and the first thing to remember is that you are not a captain, and will have to do lots of hard manual work for which a fitted waistcoat and a long sash – a liability when you are balancing on the foremast – will not be the best choice. Seafarers' dress is practical and simple: a pair of long trousers, a loose shirt and probably a handkerchief tied around the head to soak up all the sweat. Hard-wearing linen or woollen broadcloth are the best choice for your garments. Bright colours? Why not, but your clothes will get very wet, so avoid embellishments like iron buckles that will rust. Leather boots, even if you can afford them, are really only appropriate in the worst weather. Bare feet will serve you better most of the time, and you can waterproof your clothing by coating it with ship's tar. This is a common practice in the Royal Navy, and is why a sailor is known as a 'jack tar'.

↗ This illustration of Black Bart from Captain Johnson's *History of the most notorious Pyrates* shows off his flair for fashion: bedecked in ribbons and fine garments, topped off with a full tricorn hat, he was renowned as a pirate of exquisite taste – and the means to fund his habit.

Of course, often you will be operating in parts of the world that are hot and very humid, and will have to adjust your wardrobe accordingly. Many pirates abandon ordinary woollen trousers such as they would wear in wet, cold England when approaching these warmer climes, in favour of garments known as petticoat breeches. These are loose, baggy shorts with wide open legs that allow the air to circulate. Most of the time your clothing choices will be informed by such practical considerations, and if your captain is a good fellow, he will see to it that you are as well supplied with clothing as you are with food. Black Bart included new clothes in the booty list for his crew whenever they captured a ship, but remember that mending your garments will be your responsibility, so you'd best get comfortable with a needle and thread. Washing your clothes is also very important; do not model yourself on the pirates so lazy that they need a storm or a good dunking at sea to get out the grime.

Now to the accessories. Earrings are indeed popular; sailors are generally a superstitious bunch, and have got it in their heads that piercing the earlobe improves eyesight. But earrings may have a practical purpose too – it is said that sailors wear gold and silver rings in their ears so that no matter where they die, their crewmates can pay for their burial. Your captain may well wear a tricorn hat or something in keeping with his rank. For you, a woollen cap will keep you warm at night, but it will offer no protection in a fight. A bowler hat is good and solid. It offers some shade and can even absorb a spent sword stroke.

A more realistic rendering of pirate garb; in warmer climates, loose-fitting, billowing shirts and trousers will help you cope with the humidity and the heat. Should you wear a sash, it will be for the practical purpose of holding your pistols.

62

Maritime maladies

Pirate ships can be dens of filth, and a lack of basic cleanliness can make pirates very ill. Food poisoning is very common – some pirates eat charcoal to deal with the baleful effects of food that should have been thrown away long ago. Rats will often hitch a lift with a ship, and so it is common for pirate ships to be infested with them and the fleas that they bring. Rats are nature's great survivors, and somehow they will continue to multiply in spite of how many you kill. (Rats are quite like pirates, aren't they?) The captain of a Spanish galleon reported killing over 4,000 rats on a single voyage. Expect them to crawl across your face while you are in your hammock. In addition to rats, you must expect lice, which will enjoy living in your dirty clothing, and cockroaches. You will be amazed

⚥ Rats are an inevitability of life on ship. These stowaways will plague you from the very beginning of your journey, and over the course of your voyage you will find that they multiply, no matter how many you despatch!

◄◄ A man struck by delirium tremens may well convince himself that he is being followed by gorgeous mermaids; don't allow yourself to be taken in by his tales. And more importantly, avoid over-indulging in rum yourself. Drunken sailors see more mermaids than anyone else.

◄ To avoid scurvy, ensure that your ship is well stocked with citrus fruits, such as this galleon crew are loading.

to find that when you are in the Caribbean your ship will be crawling with cockroaches, but when you reach colder climes on the way back to Europe they will all suddenly die and you can sweep their little corpses into the sea. When any of these beasts bite you, you risk catching 'the itch', a disease that doctors call scabies.

Many pirates wear their clothes until they are nothing but rags, and the same is true for bandages, prolonging the vicious cycle of sickness. Here follow the most common diseases that you are likely to encounter:

DELIRIUM TREMENS
This is a condition characterized by hallucinations, in other words, seeing things that aren't really there. Men so afflicted will often claim to have been visited by beautiful mermaids – as if the sea dogs should be so lucky. Avoid over-indulging in drink if you want to keep your wits about you – this very serious condition is one of the nastier symptoms of withdrawal after a heavy period of alcohol consumption.

SCURVY

You will know that you have scurvy when your teeth start falling out, your skin goes very pale, your legs get very fat and you have to keep racing off to the pissdale. It was once very common for sailors to contract scurvy on long sea voyages, but in recent years it has been discovered that it can be staved off by eating fruits high in vitamin C, like lemons and limes.*

* NOTE FROM THE EDITOR: In 1795 the British Royal Navy started giving lime juice to its sailors to ward off scurvy, which is why the Americans call them the Limeys.

LOCKJAW

This is a strange and mysterious condition of which we know little. The mouth goes into a spasm so that it cannot be opened, so that the afflicted can neither speak nor eat. You will eventually die.

DRY BELLY ACHE

Dry belly ache, or 'painter's colic', is an awful feeling in the stomach. I have heard it suggested that this is caused by lead poisoning, whatever that is.

MANIA

This condition is often known by its more common name: going mad. Months at sea can bring on mania in the most sensible man. Sufferers may start seeing things that aren't there, like mermaids. They may also become very frightened when they hallucinate and think that the ship is under attack. There is no cure, but the man must be secured in the hold until he quietens down so that he does not disturb his fellow crewmen.

⚓ A mosquito of a species indigenous to Britain, but capable of carrying the deadly fever virus that has caused misery among so many seafaring crews.

BRONZE JOHN OR YELLOWJACKET

These are our names for the deadly Yellow Fever, which begins with severe belly ache, muscle pain and headaches and then affects your liver, turning your skin yellow – hence the name. Be on guard against mosquitoes in the Spanish Main and other tropical environments to avoid this potentially fatal disease. It strikes everyone differently – you may find yourself with only a mild case, while members of your crew die around you. There is no known cure; you must simply let it run its course. Better not to contract it in the first place.

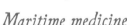

Maritime medicine

Should you find yourself afflicted by any of these illnesses, seek out the ship's surgeon – you will find his sick bay located in the bows of the ship. There may be medicine to cure whatever is wrong with you, but believe me, you are in far greater danger from accidents on board ship. Broken limbs can be caused by rolling cannons, falling cargo and the mayhem of invading other ships. Dealing with such injuries also falls to the ship's surgeon, who will even perform amputations if it is necessary. To have a limb cut off is, needless to say, not a pleasant experience. The unfortunate pirate who has to lose a leg or an arm will suffer the operation with nothing more to soothe him than a strong swig of rum, and it has to be done swiftly; a surgeon has just ten minutes before the pirate will bleed to death. He may have to chop the limb off using the edge of a sharp axe, and he will then heat up the flat side of the axe to cauterize what is left. If your ship doesn't have its own surgeon, no matter – the ship's carpenter or cook will step in; all that's needed is some confidence with a blade and a strong stomach.

Food on board

'No adventure is to be made without Belly Timber', wrote Charles Johnson in his book about pirates. 'Belly Timber' is what we call food on board, and you may not be looking forward to this aspect of the pirate life. Have you been told stories of biscuits so hard that they crack your teeth, and have to be soaked in water for hours just so you can swallow them? Have you also heard that these same biscuits get infested with weevils, so that you are likely to have a wriggly mess in your mouth? Well, stop worrying, because

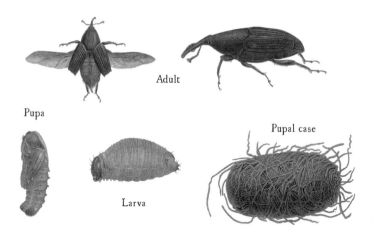

Adult

Pupa

Pupal case

Larva

⚑ Various stages in the life cycle of the palm weevil that you may find sharing your stores.

all being well, you will eat better on a pirate ship than you do on land. In extreme cases, of course, food must be improvised. One such circumstance is marooning. In 1670, Henry Morgan's men, stranded on a remote island in the Caribbean, were so hungry that they resorted to eating the leather from their satchels. One of the crew wrote that the best way to cook it was to slice it into pieces, soak it, and then beat it to tenderize it. The resulting fare could then be roasted or grilled, and eaten in very small pieces sodden with water. But I hope you will not have to try eating leather. Contrary winds, or no wind at all, can also have devastating results, paralyzing your ship on the open sea. In this scenario, the captain will usually ration the ship's supplies of food and water. In 1680, a group of buccaneers facing this predicament bought water from another ship for thirty Pieces of Eight per pint – you see how desperate a situation it is to be in! Rationing will also be put into effect if pirates miss their intended destination, as happened when Black Bart and his two ships, *Royal Fortune* and *Good Fortune*, accidentally sailed past the island where he had planned to rest and overhaul his ships. The single hogshead of water (63 gallons) didn't go far when portioned out among 130 men, and what food they had was salted, which made their thirst worse.

But don't be put off – such desperate cases are rare. Pirate captains are not stupid; they know that crewmen with full tummies are less likely to mutiny, and as you will in all likelihood not be undertaking long voyages – instead either regularly putting into port or even basing yourselves in a pirate town between raids – you will have frequent access to plentiful supplies of food. And of course, you will be intending to seize various international delicacies from the ships that you accost. Spanish crews eat particularly well, thanks to the thriving trading ports along the Spanish

↑ A rum distillery in the West Indies, 1823. Rum is a popular choice among pirates.

Main, so if you capture a Spanish ship make sure your plunder includes a few jars of their delicious olive oil.

You'll recall that the buccaneers earned their name from the food they prepared and sold to passing ships – meat, fresh from the hunt, grilled or smoked over a barbecue. Delicious! You'll need to soak the strips, smoked and dried to last at sea, for a long while before they are properly edible. Still, you will not starve, nor crack your teeth. You can always wash it down with beer – it's safer than the water – and there will be brandy in northern territories. The Americas offer plentiful supplies of rum. Most of those who sail to the West Indies (pirates included) enjoy rum punch, a mixture of rum, lime juice and sugar. If you are served something only called punch it is likely to be a mixture of brandy and water with perhaps the addition of local spices or fruit. As for wine, Madeira, otherwise known as 'Red Sack', keeps well out in the Caribbean, so there ought to be a good supply on board. Add lemon juice and spices to make sangria. You may also be offered 'flip', strong beer mixed with sugar and rum and warmed up using a hot iron. I do not recommend trying to make the buccaneers' supposed tipple of rum mixed with gunpowder – the story is complete fiction, and needless to say, such a mixture would not be good for you.

↟ Though quick and nimble swimmers, turtles on land are an easy target and a good source of delicious meat.

↘ A parrot makes a fine pet for a pirate; their colourful plumage is sure to brighten up life on ship, and they are highly sociable birds.

Have you ever tasted turtle? It's very tasy – so much so, in fact, that people have collected turtles on voyages to take back as presents for kings, only to find when the vessel docks that all the turtles have been eaten! The meat from the upper part of a turtle is called calipach, and is usually boiled to make turtle soup. Meat from the under-shell, calipee, is particularly good roasted or baked. The turtles can be kept alive on deck, so that your meat is always fresh, and their eggs are nice too. Turtles are plentiful in the Caribbean, and though they are very agile swimmers they are easy to catch on dry land. The secret is to grab hold of one and quickly turn it on its back so that it is helpless.

If your voyage does not take you into turtle territory, you can expect to be treated to beef, pork and lots of fish. Boiled shark is also rather good. You may not eat many potatoes while at sea, because they don't keep well, but in the tropics there is corn bread and cassava to be had, and fruit such as bananas and oranges (eat plenty of them to avoid scurvy). If you are in the right place, you might even get chocolate...

Finally, there is always Solomon Gundy, otherwise known as Salmagundi, an easy-to-make and versatile dish – a salad with meat, assembled in almost any combination you can think of. You will get used to it very quickly. A dependable supply of meat is often best assured by keeping live animals on board. Chickens can be raised in coops on the quarterdeck, while pigs, turtles and goats may be given free rein on the main deck – just be sure to clear up after them.

The considerate pirate's guide to the care and welfare of parrots

Of course, we don't just keep animals on board for the slaughter; keeping animals as pets is a good way to keep your spirits up on board. Pirates and parrots are linked in the popular imagination for good reason; to have a companion that will be loyal to you, will sit on your shoulder and which you can teach to talk is indeed a pleasant diversion from the hard work of crewing a pirate ship. Parrots will also provide entertainment for your mates, and that will make you a popular fellow; these sociable birds like people, so they won't attack the crew, and they are well suited to life on the ship – they enjoy flying around and resting in the rigging. They don't eat very much, which is useful in times of hardship, and what they do eat can be easily stored on board. Nuts are essential to their diet, but they will also appreciate fruit if you have it. Tropical fruits may be found in abundance along the Spanish Main, but never feed a parrot an avocado – they are poisonous to the birds. Conversely, because parrots are small creatures, no one will want to eat your pet when food is scarce. The best places to find parrots are the wild, uninhabited islands off Africa and South America that you visit. There are over 300 different parrot species, but my favourite is the macaw. These highly intelligent birds love nothing more than being taught tricks and learning to speak. A healthy macaw can live for up to thirty years. If well treated, your pet will settle on your shoulder, making you look like a real pirate. Pirates will also often keep a ship's cat to catch mice and rats, but make sure that the cat does not kill your parrot. Dogs are not appropriate on board, but you might consider a pet monkey. A monkey would have fitted in quite well with many crews I have known.

The regretful pirate's guide to tattoos

It is not just parrots that people associate with pirates. Once it is known that you have become a pirate, everyone will ask to see your tattoos; but here I wish to sound a note of caution. If you have a tattoo on your shoulder instead of a parrot, remember that it will be there for ever. Did you acquire it during a rather lively night out in Port Royal? (Can you even remember choosing the design?) Bear in mind that a distinctive tattoo is an identifying mark that could be very useful to the authorities if you are arrested by the watch. It will be no good claiming that you are not who they think you are if you have your own name tattooed upon your back. But if you are set on the idea, then what to get? A simple anchor design is quite common, but to add 'Death to the French!' in bold letters might seem foolhardy in hindsight if you are caught by their officers. The

most spectacular designs are worn by the pirates of Japan, who look like walking art galleries.

The dangers of the pirate life

The pirate life might seem very pleasant. Imagine the peaceful scene. You are happily settled into your ship; you know your place in the crew, you have managed to avoid getting scurvy or falling beneath a wayward cannon, and you have a parrot perched atop your tastefully tattooed shoulder. But this can change rapidly, so do not drop your guard – the ocean contains many hidden dangers.

For example, ten feet beneath the waters at the southern tip of the Caribbean island Las Aves is a three-mile-long reef. At night it is hidden from view, and after dark on 11 May 1678 a French fleet approached the island. The submerged rocks and coral crushed the bow of the first ship as if it were as fragile as an eggshell. Men lost their footing. Rigging and spars toppled onto the deck. In just thirty seconds, the flagship was destroyed. Perhaps Dr Samuel Johnson said it best: 'being in a ship is being in a gaol, with the chance of being drowned'.

↟ The tattoos worn by Japanese pirates are remarkably intricate, elegant designs.

You might not expect it, but fire is also a great danger. Ships are made of wood and there is plenty of tar, hemp, and cloth lying about – all of which burns easily. Throw in some gunpowder and you have a very dangerous situation. A careless smoking pirate, a stray ember from the galley or a knocked-over candle can ignite a fierce fire. William Snelgrave, a prisoner aboard the *Windham* galley in 1719, recalls an occasion during his captivity when a seaman was drawing rum from a barrel when a lit candle dropped through the bunghole. The rum caught fire, which soon spread to a second barrel. They exploded, but thankfully the fire didn't reach the nearby stores of pitch and tar, which would surely have spelled destruction for the ship. No wonder seamen fear fire.

A SUDDEN STORM

You are sailing along with a following wind, a blue sky and the deeper blue of the sea. The sun is shining and you feel the warmth on your skin as you balance on the yardarm while neatly furling the sails. Yes, it can be as idyllic as it sounds, but then, with almost no warning, total darkness hits you as the clouds thicken, blotting out the sun. The winds rise to churn the still waters into choppy seas that erupt suddenly with mountains of angry waves. The rigging will be wet and slippery and the deck will be treacherous to walk on. The wind will slam the rain into your face like tiny stones. Then the great waves will begin to hit you, sweeping the ship up at forty-five degrees and then crashing it down again with a force that will jar every bone in your body. This is how quickly the sea can turn on you. Everything on deck

⸸ Painting of a Dutch vessel that has not survived a violent turn in the weather. The convoy in the background offers some hope to any straggling survivors; a lone ship has no such safety net.

must be lashed down so that it is neither washed overboard nor flung from one side to another, smashing anything – and anyone – in its path. Here, discipline is essential. You will never be colder and never wetter. Hang on to anything you can for dear life! Sailing through a storm can terrify even the most experienced pirate. Yards, sheets, braces and rigging can be ripped away as if someone has taken an axe and cut them down. Men can be tossed across the slippery deck or flung overboard, and if a pirate falls overboard, he will probably drown – a ship cannot stop easily, and chances are that by the time the crew has manoeuvred her to retrace her path, even if the waters have calmed, the man will already be lost to the sea.

THAT SINKING FEELING

Fortunately, the sinking of a ship is actually quite a rare event; holes from cannonballs are unlikely to create a large enough breach to bring a vessel down, and rarely does a fire rage so fiercely that it causes the downfall of a ship. But a ship may be so severely battered by a storm that almost nothing of it is left. That really will be a shipwreck. In the event that your ship does go under, cling onto anything that floats. You do know how to swim, don't you? When in the water there are two main hazards. The first is freezing to death in a cold sea. Drowsiness will sweep over you before you drown. In warmer waters, the danger is from sharks, against whom there is no defence. If the storm occurs anywhere near land, you may be so lucky as to wash up on the shore – but you could also be smashed upon rocks.

PREDICTING CALAMITY

How to avoid such catastrophes? Simple: watch out for omens suggesting bad luck. When you prepare for your departure, check your calendar; sailors prefer not to set sail on Fridays, and to sail on Friday the thirteenth will double a voyage's misfortune. The seventeenth and the twenty-ninth of any month, however, are good days to set sail.

When you traverse the southern seas, you will encounter the albatross; stories tell us that these birds are the restless souls of dead sailors, and woe betide any pirate who kills one, for a storm will surely strike to avenge it. To avert disaster, you must tie the bird's carcass around the murderer's neck and lash him to the mainmast, where he will stay without food or drink until the storm ends. One should also be wary of storm petrels, otherwise known as 'Mother Carey's chickens', a name thought to stem from the Mother of God, who protects sailors and sends these birds to warn us of coming storms. These birds, like the albatross, contain the souls of dead comrades, so to kill one is to kill a fellow mariner, and any sailor who does so will die.

Sharks and turtles are also associated with bad luck. You may dine on turtles, but if you kill one and don't eat it that is very bad luck; if, however, you carry a turtle bone in your pocket, you will enjoy good luck.

If sharks follow in the wake of a ship, it means that someone on board will soon die – they are patiently waiting for their meal to be consigned to its fate. Manta rays are as unlucky as sharks, for sailors believe that these creatures can attach themselves to a ship's anchor and drag the vessel under the waves.

⚓ Blue sharks circle this sinking ship; a desperate situation for the survivors.

⤆ This illustration from Samuel Taylor Coleridge's *The Rime of the Ancient Mariner* shows the penance of a man believed to have brought misfortune on his crew by killing an albatross.

Sea-going vessels often have a figurehead adorning the bow. It is believed that a ship cannot sink as long as the figurehead remains attached. During a fierce storm, legend tells us, the tempest would abate if a woman bared her breasts. This is why ship's figureheads are often carved into the shape of bare-breasted women.

Legend also says that Saint Erasmus, also known as Saint Elmo, died during a sea storm. Just before his demise, he promised the crew he would return and show himself in some form if they were to survive the tempest. Not long after, the sailors saw a mysterious light at the masthead of their vessel and assumed Erasmus had kept his word that they would not drown.

This is why the bright lights sometimes seen around a ship's masts and yards during a storm are called Saint Elmo's Fire – though some

🦶 The phenomenon known as Saint Elmo's Fire lighting a ship's masthead during a storm.

people will tell you they are caused by lightning. Sailors believe the Fire's appearance is a sign that the worst of the storm is over, and that as long as the light remains high among the masts, luck will follow. But if it shines on the deck, bad luck is certain, and if the light appears round a man's head he will soon die. So you see, you are in superstitious company among sailors.

WHAT TO DO WHEN YOU THINK YOU SEE A MERMAID

Of all the strange sights you may see when you are on a long voyage, the most remarkable will be a mermaid. A mermaid will typically appear as a beautiful young woman with long blonde hair and full breasts. Below the waist, however, she will be a fish, and the bad news doesn't end there: mermaids are traditionally associated with dangerous events such as storms, drownings or shipwrecks. The sight of a mermaid may, therefore, be a warning of something horrible to come. Alternatively, you may simply fall in love with her, although I do not think that has ever happened to a fierce pirate. The famous Christopher Columbus reported a sighting of three mermaids in 1493. He wrote that they were not as beautiful as he had expected, however, so he may just have seen a creature like a large seal from a distance. Blackbeard, for all his ferocity, was a firm believer in mermaids, and during several voyages he instructed his crew to keep away from certain areas that were enchanted by mermaids who would bring only bad luck.

4
The Practical Pirate

S o now you know what you are letting yourself in for. You have what it takes to become a pirate, you know where you fit in and what the dangers are, so let's get down to some practicalities. We will begin with the pirate ship. For any pirate, the ship is the most vital piece of equipment, and you need to know as much about ships as is possible.

The pirate ship: a consumer's guide

Will you sail in a humble merchantman, snatched from a lone trader in some quiet strait, or do you have your heart set on commanding the most intimidating man-of-war to scourge the seas? There are nearly as many types of ship are there are types of pirate – so read on and see which calls to you!

THE SAILING SHIP
Your pirate ship will probably be a sailing ship, propelled by the wind – and this determines all aspects of ship design and pirating strategy that you will ever have to grapple with. In an ideal world (and oftentimes

your world will be far from ideal), the first thing to look for in choosing a pirate ship is its speed. Look for a vessel that is sleek and slim, cutting through the waves like a knife through gruel. A fast pirate ship will outsail any sluggish merchantman and outrun heavy warships, outweighing any disadvantages pertaining to your light ship's lack of resistance to cannon fire.

⚓ English two-masted sloops travelling in convoy – the best defence against pirates like you!

You will, of course, have cannons of your own, but take on no more than you need – their weight will slow you down, and you cannot fight and capture ships if you can't catch up to them. But do not assume that you will be firing heavy broadsides and sinking ships all the time. In fact, you are likely to make more successful raids if your ship looks small and defenceless, concealing its true potency until the last moment – surprise is a very important factor in pirate warfare. Most of the time you will seek to avoid a fight, and the good news is that most of your victims will be thinking along the same lines. If they know they cannot escape from your fast, fierce-looking vessel, they will probably surrender without firing a single shot.

← A ketch. They may be slower than other vessels, but because of this, ketches can provide the perfect disguise for a pirate vessel.

↓ A 17th-century barque longue, which you may see in the Mediterranean, as their design favours calm waters.

The best kind of sleek, swift ship I have described is a 'sloop'. Sloops are the traditional choice of privateers, who crew them with between twenty and sixty men and arm them with between ten and twenty guns, although the French favour fewer ship's guns and more hand-held muskets. There is no mistaking a sloop, because it will have one mainsail cocked at an arrogant and intimidating angle. A good example is the Rhode Island privateer sloop *Hope*, which had seven guns and attacked British vessels during the Revolutionary War. In 1780 it left Providence, Rhode Island, under Captain James Monroe and captured a British ship bound for New York that was laden with rum and sugar. When Henry Morgan sailed against Panama for his famous raid, he used a fleet of thirty-seven sloops, none of which were over-large. As well as being very fast, a sloop is easy to maintain and quite easy to obtain by legitimate means – but do not choose one that is too small for the job. A small crew may mean fewer people to share your spoils with, if you are feeling greedy, but a small crew might not give you the manpower needed for boarding, leaving you overwhelmed by the more numerous sailors on a warship.

Among the French and Dutch, I hear, there is a preference for a slightly heavier vessel called a 'barque longue'. These have two masts and additional oar propulsion, which is useful in stiller waters. As for the diminutive ship known as a 'ketch', well, they are notoriously slow and sluggish, but if you wish to disguise your true nature as a pirate ship, an innocent-looking ketch may be the best bet – chances are you will be mistaken for a humble crew of fishermen. Much less sluggish is the tough 'flyboat', or 'flute', which is typically a cargo-carrying vessel. The great Blackbeard's flute, *Queen Anne's Revenge,* fought off a much larger ship, although many will tell you that flyboats are no good in a pursuit situation. Duguay-Trouin once remarked that he sailed a flute for three months and took no prizes apart from a Spanish ship that was heavily laden with sugar, in his eyes a failed expedition.

Alternatively you might choose a large, solid fighting vessel; perhaps a former man-of-war. It may not match the speed of its prey, but it will certainly pack a punch at close quarters. Sneaking up on your victim is, therefore, essential in such a ship. Often a privateer's sponsor, keen that there be sufficient space for all the pirate loot that the mission is expected to bring home, will obtain one as part of his commission. Otherwise a pirate captain might capture such a vessel, transferring his colours to it. Some pirates also make this decision for themselves. The corsairs of St Malo, of northern France, for example, regularly use ships with fifty or more guns because of the firepower, which they value more than speed – not to mention it can be very prestigious to sail in such a vessel. The St Malo pirates, of course, have a safe harbour nearby to return to. You may not be so fortunate, and a large ship obviously cannot be hidden in a small creek.

Pirates often get little choice about what sort of vessel they have and must make do with whatever comes their way, but the good news is that almost anything can be adapted and improved to suit your needs. So, for example, if you have captured a really fine, large warship you might wish to remove all unnecessary ornamentation, such as elaborate carvings, and cut down the size of various roundhouses and quarterdecks, in order to improve its speed. You can reduce the weight of cannons by swapping them for light swivel guns mounted on the ship's sides. Having said that, when it comes to using a ship as a fighting machine, size does matter, even though numerous cannons place a huge strain on a vessel. There is first of all the weight itself, which can cause cracks in the planking – with obvious disastrous consequences – but worse still is what can happen in rough seas, when the cannons start to move about and may even snap their ropes. A sudden shift of their weight to one side can cause a ship to capsize. Gun ports can also be a real menace in a swell, allowing the entry of water that might dampen the gunpowder, rendering it useless. That is why gun ports are usually caulked shut until the very last moment, when you are ready to open fire in battle (which also gives the advantage of surprise by making your victim think that you have fewer guns than you actually possess).

⚓ A junk from the eastern seas of China. These vessels are often elaborately painted, and so are beautiful as well as being well built and functional.

Finally, don't pour scorn on the type of vessel you will meet in the Far East. The most commonly used word to describe any East Asian ship is 'junk', but it doesn't mean rubbish. This familiar expression was first written in English in 1555, and is probably derived from a mishearing of *chuan*, the Chinese word for boat or ship. Unfortunately, the rotten connotations of 'junk', in the English language at least, have tended to lead to a presumption that Asian ships are somehow inferior to Western ones. Yet in many respects Chinese ships are years ahead of their European counterparts. Why, some Chinese ships even have watertight compartments, so that if the junk is holed the sea will not flood the whole hull. What an idea!

THE OARED GALLEY

You are unlikely to meet an oared galley these days, but they once dominated the Mediterranean waters, and were so well suited to piracy that the overall design has changed little over 2,000 years. A galley possessed

two triangular-shaped sails, but because calm weather bedevilled sea travel it was the vessel's oars that provided the main means of propulsion. Between twenty-five and thirty oars lay on either side of the ship, each pulled by three or four oarsmen seated on – and sometimes chained to – their benches, with a narrow walkway running down the middle of the deck. A typical galley might be crewed by as many as 400 men, of whom 250 would be oarsmen, with fighting men crammed into every other square inch of the ship. Most oarsmen were prisoners who had been captured in previous battles, but there was hope for these unwilling shipmates – a chained man might have his shackles released when battle threatened, and would be promised his freedom in return for loyal service during the fight. In ancient times, galleys attacked each other by ramming or boarding, but by the middle of the fifteenth century, ships were beginning to receive extra offensive armament: breech-loading cannons mounted at the bow (the front) or the stern (the rear).

⚓ A 16th-century galley ship. The oars made them ideal for sailing in windless regions.

🛶 Small boats, such as canoes, will prove necessary for raiding ashore and approaching larger vessels before boarding.

Of course, oars have not been entirely consigned to history. They can be useful if you have a light ship and there is no wind to allow you to pursue or escape, but they are difficult to use in heavy seas. Rowing is hard work, and you must be prepared to do it, but don't worry, we don't go in for galley slaves any more!

THE WAR CANOE

The above ships sound rather grand, so it may surprise you to read that as a pirate you may end up paddling a canoe. These are generally used by pirates who raid from within the safety of a river system, especially in North and South America, and have no need to head for the open seas. Instead they make swift excursions out of a jungle-covered estuary against any enemy ship that is passing by. Sometimes the boats used for this purpose are simple dugout canoes, and very effective they are too, but big canoes can carry over twenty men for a raid, and very large varieties up to one hundred! When Europeans use them, they are rowed much like a Viking ship, rather than being paddled as is the way of native Americans. Many a pirate began his career in charge of a vessel as small as this!

Small boats also have their place on a large pirate ship. These light craft, generally carried on or even towed behind the large vessel, are

normally used for attacking unsuspecting merchantmen or to provide the transport for a raid ashore. Regardless of their use in warfare, small boats are essential equipment on any large vessel. Routine tasks such as fetching food and water, ferrying people ashore or looking for a man overboard (which is almost routine on some voyages!) would be impossible without them.

Sailing: the basics

Sailing is a fine art, and I see no need to confuse you at this stage of your education by going into all the details. You will learn all of that, and the related jargon, when you first go on board, and if you don't pick it up straight away, there will no doubt be a helpful bosun at hand ready to clip you round the ears. You will always work as part of a team and it will be many years before you really appreciate the significance of the small role you have to play in the overall sailing of the ship. When you are standing on a rope forty feet up, soaking wet, freezing to death in a howling gale, comfort yourself with this encouraging thought: 'The ship won't sail without me!'

One of the most crucial jobs on board is that of the helmsman. Nowadays the helmsman will

⚓ A helmsman steering his ship through a rough storm.

⚓ A group of pirates in a small, one-masted ship approach a Spanish galleon in this painting from Pyle's *Book of Pirates*. The treasure ship might be converted for use as a pirate ship.

steer the ship using a wheel, where a mechanical system adds force to the rudder, but before that it was with a tiller, which worked like a very large lever. Operating the tiller was very hard work, requiring several men to apply sufficient pressure in a tight move. It is no compensation for the skilled helmsman to know that he is a prime target for enemy marksmen as he stands there unprotected. Helmsmen are often shot dead by musketeers stationed in the enemy ship's rigging.

Careening and other maintenance issues

You will often find yourself having to chase your prey, and in such circumstances speed is vital. Essential to achieving this is a smooth, clean hull free of marine growths that would slow the ship down by increasing water resistance and drag. The process of scrubbing the hull of such oceanic debris is known as careening, and a good captain will careen his ship as often as possible. This is easier said than done, because you must be on dry land – unless you have worked out how to breathe underwater. Pirates can't use dry docks in naval harbours, and it would in any case be a huge risk to leave your ship so defenceless, so choose a secluded bay where you are likely to remain undetected. Work out the timing of the tides and allow the ship to be beached. Then use ropes to pull her gently onto her side, and get to work. Seaweed and barnacles have to be scraped off, and once you are down to the bare timbers, maintenance can take place. Boil some tar and use tarred rope to fill any gaps in the planking, while your carpenters replace any timber that is too damaged to be salvaged. Be sure to mount an armed guard, because your ship will be a sitting duck. Some pirates, in fact, careen only one side of a ship per visit, just to be careful. On top of careening, making sure that your ship is trim will ensure a better speed. Check your ballast – get rid of what you can – and make sure that your cargo is evenly distributed so that the ship sails smoothly through the water.

«« Putting ashore offers not only an opportunity to enjoy the spoils of piracy, but also to undertake vital maintenance on your ship, such as careening, which the pirate captain here oversees.

BILGE

One of the most fearful elements of ship maintenance has to do with the bilge, a word with two meanings. The first refers to the place at the very bottom of the ship, also known as 'the damp', where all sorts of filth accumulates. The second refers to the filth itself, which is washed down there by the scrubbing of decks, the waves of the sea washing over the ship or by the inevitable trickle of urine from the various livestock on deck. When you wash your clothes, the dirty water will end up in the bilge, along with food waste, blood, dead rats and poo. Captain Johnson wrote a vivid account of the bilge in his ship:

> This night two of our carpenter's crew being sent down to search the well were struck dead with the damp, as they call it, but being hoisted up again speedily, they recovered with much difficulty. The occasion of these damps is the tightness of the ship and, lying still a long time, the bilge water corrupts and stinks, so that it is enough to poison the devil, and all the little plate and silver I had hath been turned black with the vapours of our bilge water in a night time.

So the stench from the bilge is so powerful that it can make crewmen faint – these poor pirates had to be dragged back up by their mates – and the chemicals coming off it will turn silver black overnight! How to ensure you never have to encounter such a harrowing mess? For starters, you can avoid adding to the problem. On board the toilet is known as the 'head', since it sits up in the bow of the ship. If your ship has bulwarks – defensive extensions of the hull – there may an additional facility there, known, appropriately, as the pissdale. If you don't fancy squatting in either, you could simply hang onto the rigging and stick your bottom over the side (though this is not advised when the sea is running a swell and the waves are beating up against your bare bum). Just remember that should you drop your trousers carelessly aboard ship it will all end up in the bilge, and you may be the one who is given the job of pumping it out again.

Selecting your arsenal

FIREPOWER

So, you have your ship and you know how to keep it in good nick. Now how to use it to best effect in your quest to become the most obscenely wealthy captain of the seas? Fill it with terrifying, devastating weapons, of course, and learn how to wield them most fearsomely.

If I was to ask which weapon you most associate with a pirate ship, I would expect the answer 'a cannon', because the idea of a ship engaging with another with all guns blazing is a very popular one. Though you will not always want to resort to using them, there will certainly be heavy-calibre guns of some sort on your ship. A ship's cannon is typically a heavy barrel of iron or bronze, the latter being lighter and more manoeuvrable, although more expensive. Two centuries ago, different sizes of cannon were given confusing names, like sakers and culverins, but nowadays we tend to classify them according to the weight of the shot (cannonballs) they fire, from three pounds up to twenty-four pounds and even larger. Three-, four- and six-pound-shot cannons are favoured by English privateers commanding sloops, whereas the heavier-calibre guns are better suited to large men-of-war and some big merchant vessels, which may be converted into pirate ships by their new owners.

A ship's cannons will each be mounted on a gun carriage with two sets of wheels, known as trucks. The rear wheels are smaller than those at the front, to allow the carriage to remain horizontal in spite of the curvature of the deck. The curve of the deck, which is upwards toward the centre, also assists in absorbing recoil – the reaction of the gun to the firing that causes it to move backwards. Ropes are threaded through holes in the carriage to allow the gun to be quickly restored to its firing position after it has recoiled. All cannons can, and do, fire cannonballs (otherwise known as 'round shot'), although that is not always the best choice of projectile to stick down a barrel – a small, six-pound shot will

⚓ A ship's cannon, the most formidable weapon on board, loaded on its gun carriage and affixed to the ship by a system of ropes, blocks and pulleys.

←« One of the most useful types of firearm for a pirate is the light swivel gun. Their great advantage is that they are breech-loading, which makes up for some leakage around the barrel and a lower impact. They are often mounted at the stern of the ship, but in this picture they are being used as coastal defences.

simply bounce off the hull of a really strong vessel. Sometimes cannons are double-shotted; in other words, two balls are loaded simultaneously. This widens the target area of a single blast, but reduces its striking power, split across the two projectiles. If your target is not the planking of the ship but the ropes of the rigging, you could use a 'double-head', otherwise known as a 'double-end shot': two single shots or two half-shots fastened together with an iron bar. 'Chain shot' is very similar – the connecting device is an iron chain. You can imagine what either of those will do to ropes, rigging, sails or even a person. A double-head is also a good choice if you wish to disable an enemy's rudder; a direct hit might splinter it, rendering it useless for steering and so paralyzing your foe. There are also various sorts of shot that have been deliberately designed to kill people, generally engineered so that many small pieces of iron are fired at once and spread out in flight, like buckshot from a hand-held blunderbuss (a wide-mouthed musket). These weapons are easy to improvise in a pinch. You just fill a tin or a cloth bag with musket balls, shards of iron, scrap metal or even small, sharp stones. This mixture tends to go by the name of 'case shot', or 'canister', and can be very effective against rigging as well.

Swivel guns are the smaller weapons mounted on the ship's rails, and these are very different from the larger ship's cannons. The most popular place to mount them is in the stern. Early European swivel cannons were built from wrought iron, made from staves hammer-welded together and strengthened by hoops, just like a wooden barrel, a process which may well explain the use of the term 'barrel' for a gun. The 'swivel' of the swivel gun is the pivot that allows it to rotate and be elevated. Some swivel guns are muzzle-loaded, which means that the shot is fed into the mouth of the cannon, but others are loaded from the breech end – that is, the rear end of the chamber. These models are thus called breech-loaders. The gunpowder and wad are combined inside a sturdy container shaped like a large tankard and placed into the breech end along with the shot, a metal or wooden wedge is driven in behind the removable breech to make as tight a fit against the barrel opening as can reasonably be expected, and then the gun is fired. Breech-loaders are popular in naval warfare because they do not need to be hauled back into the ship to be swabbed out. The gun is simply rotated. They can also be reloaded quickly. The main disadvantage is leakage around the muzzle and a consequent loss of explosive energy, but this is compensated for by the comparatively high rate of fire. A different type of swivel gun is an 'espingole', which is essentially a large fat musket permanently mounted on the ship's rail. Some ships are even known to have mortars, which are short, fat cannons that fire a ball or an explosive shell on a high trajectory. These can be very useful if attacking a fort from the sea.

SWORDS AND CUTLASSES: CHOOSE YOUR WEAPON

You cannot subdue an enemy ship through firepower alone. The time will come to board the ship and claim your prizes – but do not expect to do so unopposed! You will need to be prepared to enter into close combat,

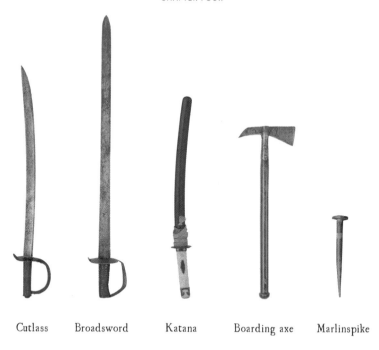

Cutlass   Broadsword   Katana   Boarding axe   Marlinspike

and in this a variety of weapons will prove useful, provided you know how to use them. You will certainly have heard of the cutlass, the sword that is associated with pirates as is no other weapon. It has a short blade, making it ideal for use in the confined space and press of a boarding raid, and its strong protective hilt will keep your hands safe from cuts as well. But you will need to practise before picking up your cutlass. I recommend starting with a cudgel, a short, stout stick. Practise hitting with something like that, which is heavy and made of wood, and remember that the cutlass is an edged weapon that will cut as well as bash. But mastering your attack is not enough; your enemy will also be trying to strike you! So leave room for defensive strokes. Try and grab his sword arm with your free hand, or kick him. You may, of course, be attacked by lots of people – an enemy ship is hardly a gentleman's duelling yard – so envisage swinging your cutlass round your head, taking down anyone who comes near.

When you are promoted to the rank of captain, you will probably wish to wield a proper sword, as befits your standing. This is fully understandable, but you will have to acquire real swordsmanship skills through long practice at fencing. The French corsair Duguay-Trouin was a superlative swordsman; he was often the first among his crew to board an enemy ship and once wounded an enemy captain in a sword fight before capturing his vessel. Duguay-Trouin favoured a sabre, so take heed of the example set by an expert. A rapier? With its long blade used for thrusting, a rapier is not the best thing for a ship because of the tight squeeze when you are fighting. You may find yourself too cramped up against your enemies to use it effectively, and the only realistic recourse is then to jab with it like a spear. A scimitar? That is the curved-blade sword favoured by Muslims. You may have encountered one if you have been active in the Mediterranean, and they certainly offer a promising alternative to the cutlass. A Scottish broadsword? Its massive blade can cause a lot of damage, but in untrained hands and a confined space you would be as likely to hurt your own men as the enemy. The most deadly swords of all are the dreadful Japanese samurai swords that the *wako* carried, but you are unlikely to meet them, I'm glad to say.

When you read later about boarding parties, I will refer to the use of a 'boarding axe'. These are mainly used for smashing your way into a closed cabin or cutting rigging rather than in combat, but in a pinch one may be as effective as a cutlass. You will always keep a knife on you, but expect to use it as a tool – although again, if you lose your cutlass, a knife will come in very handy for fighting. You could even carry one in your non-sword hand when fighting with a cutlass. The best use of a knife is as a concealed weapon for sneaking up on someone, but may I make one suggestion? Whatever you may have heard about pirates in stories, don't carry your knife with the blade clenched in your mouth. It won't help you in a fight and can be very bad for your teeth – and even more so for your tongue.

Do you want something with a longer reach? Boarding pikes, javelins and even muskets with fitted bayonets are useful longer-range weapons.

You may also wonder if you should be wearing armour. An old breastplate can stop a musket ball, so these are popular among captains and helmsmen, who are likely to find themselves the centre of the enemies' attention. John Paul Jones liked body armour, which suited his reckless approach, but in a hand-to-hand fight you may find that heavy, bulky armour is an unnecessary hindrance.

You may also have heard of pirates fighting with something called a marlinspike. Strictly speaking, a marlinspike is not a weapon; it is a tool used for unravelling ropes. But it has a sharp spike, so if crewmen are feeling mutinous, and the captain has locked all conventional weapons away, they may well lay their hands on marlinspikes as a last resort.

MUSKETS, AND HOW TO FIRE ONE

The flintlock musket was the weapon of choice among the early bucca-neers of the Spanish Main, particularly those who had no cannons on their ships. The buccaneers were good shots because of the practice they had hunting wild pigs. If your muskets are wielded by sharpshooters as good as them, you can clear an enemy's decks as efficiently as with any massive broadside cannon. The ultimate use of muskets in this manner is for a crack-shot to shoot dead the helmsman (and anyone who replaces him), or even the enemy captain. Twenty skilled men with muskets will do more harm to an enemy ship than the same number of six-pound shots. Their accurate fire will also cause more havoc and considerably more fear.

You may also encounter an older type of musket called an 'arquebus' or 'matchlock', but I wouldn't recommend them. They worked by drop-ping a lighted match, held in a frame called a serpentine, directly onto the powder – and who wants a smouldering match burning where there is powder about? Flintlocks are much safer. In these models, flint hits the metal above the touch hole, providing the spark that will ignite the powder inside. The smaller type of flintlocks can easily be held in the arm, but there are larger versions too: one is even called a buccaneer gun. They

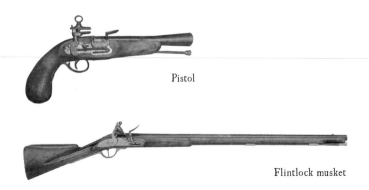

Pistol

Flintlock musket

are easy to aim and fire, but a rest is recommended, or at least somewhere to place the heavy barrel. The opposite extreme is the blunderbuss, which has a short barrel and a wide muzzle. The shot is spread like case shot: very useful in close-quarter boarding fights.

If you become a ship's musketeer, you will need to be able to load your gun successfully under pressure in the heat of battle, and in this our modern times make us very fortunate, because of the invention of bullet cartridges. In the olden days, you had to pour loose gunpowder from a powder horn into the musket's barrel, followed by wadding and the bullet. Everything then had to be rammed down, and extra powder put into the vent. You would need to be equipped with a good, strong ramrod; if it were to break inside the barrel, you would be in considerable danger. The whole loading process took a lot of time. But nowadays, you will use prepared cartridges made of paper that already contain both the bullet and the right amount of gunpowder. The paper acts as the wadding, to ensure that the bullet is a tight fit behind the charge. Some buccaneers speed the loading process even further by banging the butt of their musket on the ground. This forces enough powder back into the vent to take the spark, so no extra priming powder needs to be added to the touch hole.

The effective range of a musket is quite short; really no more than 250 yards. This should be close enough to kill a man, provided you are smack on target, but take the example of Captain Davis, who took four musket shots to his body when he was fighting the Portuguese. A fifth shot felled him, but his enemies cut his throat just to make sure he was in fact dead. Needless to say, firing from a rolling ship adds a whole new dimension of possible inaccuracy. You will be moving, and so will your target. Captain Nathaniel Uring, an English merchant, had a lucky escape when a French privateer's musketeer on a rolling ship fired seven shots at him – and all of them missed. Had he been in calmer waters, he would probably have been killed. You could, of course, try putting two bullets in per fire, or even using buckshot, which spreads out and is pretty much guaranteed to hit something, even if not fatally. You must always keep your weapons clean so that they remain operational, although smart pirates deliberately let brass fittings grow tarnished so that light does not reflect off them and disclose the shooter to their prey, human or animal. But watch out for rust. You will be punished by your captain if your firearm is dirty or rusty, because holding a useless weapon in battle could put your shipmates at risk.

PISTOLS

Pistols are a very effective close-range weapon. Pistols are like small muskets, and just like muskets you fire them once and then they have to be reloaded. Of course, during a boarding raid, there will be no time to reload, so a discharged pistol is then of little use, except as a club. Some pirates therefore carry several pistols at their belts or slung round their shoulders. Blackbeard is supposed to have always had six fastened about his person, and would discharge them in turn before engaging enemies with his cutlass. I have heard of pirates who fire their pistols and then throw them at the enemy, which I consider to be a waste of a good pistol. Why not just secure them by a silken string around your body like Blackbeard? Good pistols are hard to find and very expensive.

Explosive ingenuity

The pirate crews of India, China and Japan have their own distinctive weapons. Some still use bows and arrows, and do not underestimate these old-fashioned weapons – in the time it takes to reload a musket, a good archer can loose twelve shafts against you, and Japanese pirates have even perfected fire arrows. They have even developed a wide-bore musket that dispatches wooden fire arrows with leather wings –

and remember the disaster fire can spell for a ship. Trained archers are difficult to find nowadays, which is why Western pirates favour guns. In addition to bows, guns, swords and spears, Eastern crews use a variety of clever weapons. Particularly ingenious are their grappling weapons, long poles fitted with hooks

↑ A simple example of a grenade that could be thrown on to the deck of a ship. Some were loaded with substances that produced deadly fumes: tar, sulphur, coal dust, mercury and other noxious materials.

and barbed spikes with which an enemy can be seized from a distance. Some are like spears, but with very long blades and two cross blades pointing down towards the shaft like two sickles. Another type has three straight spikes barbed like fish-hooks. A polearm with a 'bear's paw' of spikes is a similar device, but bristling with spikes. Both are mounted on long shafts. Finally, we may note the 'sleeve entangler'. A mass of spikes constitute the head, and about eight inches of the upper shaft is also covered with spikes. Stay well clear of a Japanese war junk!

Both the Chinese and the Japanese are especially adept at making explosives. The main use we make of gunpowder is as a propellant for shooting cannonballs out of a gun barrel, but gunpowder can also be used to make exploding bombs. These consist of two hollow iron hemi-spheres, filled with gunpowder and numerous pieces of scrap iron, fastened together and wrapped in layers of heavy Japanese paper. A fuse, timed according to its length, runs into the interior, and a rope or cord is attached to the outside so that the bomb can be whirled around the head, picking up momentum before being loosed upon its victims. They are used both as anti-personnel weapons and as incendiary devices to sink wooden ships.

We use a similar device, although not so extensively. We call them grenades. They are thrown onto the enemy's deck and explode upon impact, sending pieces of hot metal far and wide. It is best to keep them in a secure box on your deck, ready for the assault, although the most daring soldiers call themselves grenadiers and carry the hand-thrown bombs in a pouch on their person. They tear open the protective cover of the fuse with their teeth, light it and then throw the bomb as far as they can. This is a risky business. Even more

⁑ The chaos that Greek Fire can cause on board.

dangerous are improvised bombs – glass bottles filled with gunpowder and shards of metal. These are difficult to throw with any accuracy, but ideal for dropping through a loophole or a hatch.

The crews who fought during the later Roman Empire made great use of a concoction called Greek Fire, which was made from a black, oily substance found in certain places in Arabia (the precise recipe was guarded closely – so closely, it has been lost altogether). You may see variations on this nowadays, and it is widely feared, for this oily fire cannot be put out using water. In fact, it seems to float on the surface of the sea while still burning fiercely. As we have no access to this natural oil, the best we can do is make 'fire pots' – clay containers filled with flammable material, which are thrown onto the deck of an enemy ship. If they are made with the right balance of pitch and dried materials, they can start a good fire on board. A more novel alternative is the 'stink pot', which is filled not with incendiary materials but with foul-smelling ingredients such as animal dung, sure to distract and disgust your foes.

Now you know which weapons we pirates favour and how to use them; so let's see how they can be brought into action when you are attacking a ship or raiding ashore.

5
The Pirate in Action

The day has come. You have grafted for months, practising with your cudgel in your spare moments between scrubbing the decks and navigating the rigging, and finally you spot it – a ship on the horizon, ripe for the taking. Alert your captain! Time to claim your prize.

Capturing a prize on the high seas

This is the ambition that drives many a pirate's career – capturing loot by taking another ship. This is what all sea rovers do, whether they call themselves privateers, buccaneers, corsairs or just plain old pirates. But before you leap into action, you must carefully assess the safety of your own ship, because you stand to lose everything if the day goes against you. So let's take a close look at your intended target. It will almost certainly be a merchantman, and hopefully one laden with treasure, and it would be very foolish of you to assume that the captains of merchantmen take no precautions against pirate attacks. Merchantmen will regularly band together to form a convoy, which means that they sail as a group under the protection of a warship. Up to eighty ships have been known to join up in this way; such a convoy is an impressive sight. It can be very intimidating for a pirate to see such a splendid array – but it is also a great temptation. Almost all East Indies treasure ships travel under convoy protection nowadays, and it can be so effective against pirate attack that even ships from nations who wouldn't normally agree on anything have been known to form alliances. The guard-ship captains are generally savvy sailors, often experienced in beating off pirate attacks. They take particular note of the wind direction; if the convoy has sufficient numbers of guard ships,

↑ A 17th-century engraving depicting the successful capture of Spanish galleons by a Dutch West India squadron under Piet Heyn. Convoys can be taken down, if you head up one of your own.

one or two will sail to windward of the fleet (i.e. where the wind is coming from), so that they can respond quickly if a pirate ship is seen approaching from the other (the leeward) side. Others sail some distance away from the merchantmen, even over the horizon, until a pirate ship is spotted. Then they move in unexpectedly for the kill.

Pirate captains will attack a convoy, but generally only if they head a large fleet of their own, so what are you to do if you are commanding a solitary pirate ship? Perhaps the best advice is to steer well clear and seek another target instead – but there may be opportunity yet. Quite often, one or two ships in a convoy will struggle to keep up with the rest, and some may even be so foolish as to sail to windward of their fleet, making their rescue much more difficult. The secret, then, is to pick off a straggler while it is separated from the rest of the convoy. In 1637, a lone English pirate ship captained by a man whose name is lost to history captured a Spanish ship on the margins of a convoy of fifty-two ships. The English pirates gained their victory within half an hour, sailing away with their prize before the Spanish guard ships had a chance to intervene.

Sometimes, however, the guard ships hired by a convoy will turn out to be other sleek privateers – just like you – and then you may have problems. The privateer captain will have been paid very handsomely to protect the convoy, and he is not likely to allow an enemy that might interfere with his profitable task anywhere near. You would also be most unlikely to want to attack another privateer, because that would be a fight between equals – although there are records of battles between privateers, most have happened by mistake, with each crew thinking that the other looks like easy prey. Don't fall victim to this. Just tell yourself that there is much better treasure to be had elsewhere.

If you are very lucky, you may encounter a merchantman sailing on its own, but even then there are a few things you should consider before deciding to attack. The first is obvious – how to tell the difference between a merchantman and an armed naval warship. Pirating 101: do not attack a naval warship by mistake. While some merchantmen will be armed, they are unlikely to pose a great threat to you. Merchantmen crews, you see, are sailors, not soldiers. They have not been trained to fight.

Look first at the ship's decks; on a merchant vessel, they are likely to be piled high with cargo. It will take a long time to clear those decks for action, even if the crew feel up to a fight. They may well have cannons on board, but chances are they will have been stowed away to make more room for cargo, and so will also take a long time to prepare, though it is not unknown for a desperate captain to order his crew to throw some cargo overboard to make way for the guns to be run out. In any event, their guns are likely

↑ A Dutch merchantman (right) and warship (left).

to be much smaller than yours, even if you are commanding only a small sloop with swivel guns.

The merchantman captain is likely to try to outrun you in the first instance, but if you manage to catch up in your sleek sloop, he might have some trouble persuading his crew to fight; there have certainly been occasions when seamen have disobeyed orders to engage. In such a case, the captain will have no alternative but to surrender, and you may gain the added bonus of taking experienced sailors for your crew, along with the treasure. Alternatively, the captain might order his men to take up what are known as 'closed quarters'. The crew will lock themselves into secure spaces, such as cabins, counting on the pirate attackers giving up and leaving them in peace, having stripped their ship of as much of its treasure as they can carry. It is a compromise between losing their cargo and losing their lives, and it can work if the ship being attacked is a straggler from a convoy, and so can reasonably expect a guard ship to come to their rescue. A very similar tactic is to run the ship aground and hope that the pirates will sail away – defending a ship against pirates on dry land is a better bet than encountering them at sea. The pirates would need to send their crew to shore in small boats, making them much more vulnerable to what has become a defensive position. Try to see all this from the point of view of the merchantman you are attacking. Taking up arms will be their last resort.

Surprise, surprise!

Imagine the excitement on board when the shout comes down from the lookout, high up in the crow's nest: 'A sail! A sail!'

Yes, a ship has been spotted, but the cry will be 'a sail', not 'a ship', because that may be all of the ship that is visible over the horizon. You still don't know what sort of ship it is. If you are very lucky, you will have spotted the stranger with the sun behind you – a great advantage, because the potential victim may not even know that you are there. A lookout with keen eyesight will be richly rewarded by his captain. By contrast, a lookout who is tired or even drunk may mistake a large rock or a dead whale for a ship, or even spot ships that are not actually there. He won't last long in a pirate crew, although innocent mistakes can be made. The great French corsair Duguay-Trouin once saw what he thought was a convoy of fifteen Dutch merchantmen sailing through thick mist, only to discover when the fog cleared that they were all warships – so he beat a hasty retreat.

The information shouted down to the captain about how many ships have been seen can help him make a decision about how to proceed, but first the pirate ship has to move nearer to its potential prey. Once the strange ship's position has been located on the compass, a chase can begin. The most important thing now is for your captain to find out how strong the ship is, and if possible to identify it. Some merchantmen have been known to paint imitation gun ports on their sides to deter attack. It is also possible that the ship might be a friendly vessel with whom one could exchange news and information. The important thing is to be ready for anything. The ship that the lookout has spotted might be a naval warship, so the pirate ship must move into action stations immediately, in case it is attacked in return. Otherwise, the time of plunder has arrived, so the pirate ship must be transformed into a fighting machine.

Show your true colours – or not!

So what happens when you have sailed close enough to the strange ship to be able to discern its true nature? Is it a merchantman, a man-of-war or a fellow pirate vessel? If you cannot see cargo piled up on the deck, you must rely on recognizing the ship's colours, by which I mean noting what flags are being flown. It is important to know your colours. Can you recognize the flag of the East India Company? It is most unwise to attack an East India Company ship; they are well armed, used to pirates and often have substantial support. Most vital of all, you must not get your colours confused. English sailors have mistaken the French white ensign called the *pavillon blanc* for the white flag of surrender – a serious mistake to make. A similar incident occurred in 1665, when an English ship flying the white ensign was mistaken by a short-sighted French lookout for a friendly ship. This gave the English the opportunity for a surprise attack and they took the vessel just because of their victim's mistake. Dutch ships fly their own tricolor, and Spanish colours can be very elaborate. So along with keen eyesight, you need a good knowledge of the flags you might encounter.

A privateer may well be flying the colours of their sponsor; English privateers proudly fly the King's colours, although they are forbidden from doing so when in the company of ships of the Royal Navy. The buccaneers of Jamaica did this all the time. A red flag is also very common on board a pirate ship. Hoisting the red flag usually has one of two meanings. First, if the ship you are planning to attack has refused your generous offer of quarter (that is, your offer to spare the life of everyone aboard if they surrender), you hoist the red flag to show that there will be no mercy. The

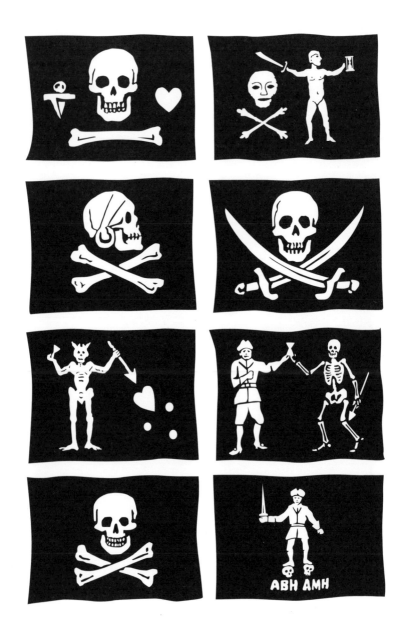

notorious Captain Kidd used only such a red flag, with nothing else on it, which became known as the 'bloody banner'. Other, more peaceful ships may once have used something similar, but nowadays the red flag always means 'pirate'. Buccaneer captains also like to have their names known, so many have their own flag designs over the red.

So who uses the most famous flag of all: the Jolly Roger? This is, of course, the famous black pirate flag with a white skull and crossbones. Well, sometimes the flag is just plain black, but Henry Avery certainly used the Jolly Roger, even embellishing the skull with a fine bandana. Black Bart went a step further; a Boston newspaper article described him sailing into a harbour in Newfoundland in a ship that flew both the English colours and a black flag with a cutlass and a 'death's head' on it at the top of the mast. He was proud to be a pirate!

But here we have a problem, for the ship may be flying false colours. Nine times out of ten, the lookout who makes the first sighting will have seen no colours at all; flying flags can slow a ship down, and they are liable to be damaged in very stormy weather. A ship will only hoist its colours when fairly close contact has been made, and so can try to deceive its foe. Perhaps the captain wants to deter attack and avoid capture by pretending to be a formidable warship; or maybe a heavily armed warship is pretending to be a weak vessel in order to entice a pirate ship to attack – and be captured. Most privateers will keep a supply of different flags on board so that they can deliberately deceive an enemy. But there are unwritten rules about how far you can push the trick, and it is a fundamental principle that whatever colours may be hoisted to deceive an enemy, an honourable pirate reveals their true colours before the attack. This can be taken to the extreme – you may have all your guns run out and ready to fire the moment the flag is flown. In this case, expect a testing shot from the other side; a demand for you to show your true colours. When the English captured Duguay-Trouin in 1694, they accused him of

◄◄◄ A collection of the fierce flags flown by pirate captains. The devil, the hourglass, the cutlass and, of course, the skull and crossbones promised a swift death to any who sighted them.

firing on them before hoisting his true colours, to which he replied that he was only showing off his strength, which may well be true. There are also many instances of pirate ships breaking the rule and attacking with no flags flying at all – we are not renowned for our honesty, after all.

As you can see, it is unwise to rely only on colours to decide a ship's intent. Most pirate captains are not fooled by flags, simply because deception is so common, and in fact this can cause problems when a ship is actually flying its true colours – it happens! The general rule is, therefore, that you should not rely on the sight of colours except when the ships are engaged in close combat, by which time it is probably too late to change your course anyway.

To chase, or not to chase?

The prize has been spotted, its colours, size and shape have been noted, and your captain has prepared the ship for action. Now will you give chase? It may instead be wiser to let the strange vessel come to you. Their crew will be as curious as you are, so why cause alarm by bearing down upon them? Instead, let them draw up close, not suspecting that yours is a pirate ship, and then hoist your true colours and let fly. You could even cheat a little (more) by pretending to be a vessel in distress, although most captains will not be fooled by that, particularly if they are sailing in waters that are known to contain pirates. Disguise is a better strategy. You can lower your topgallant masts and pretend to be a merchant ship while keeping most of the crew hidden below, which works best when you are after a real merchant ship – but it could cause problems if you encounter another privateer.

The more reckless alternative is, of course, to give chase. Drop all pretence and disguise, hope that the vessel you are after is a real merchantman, and sail straight for her. When the captain sees you bearing

⚓ A classic sea-chase: a pirate ship pursues its prey, the crew eagerly appraising their target.

down upon him in a ship made ready for action, he will know what to expect. He knows you are a pirate, whatever flag you are flying, so you might as well hoist the Jolly Roger from the start. Bolder captains might put out all the sail they have and bear down upon you in turn, trying to scare you away. Otherwise, the chase is on, and much will depend upon the relative skills possessed by the two captains in the matter of sailing their ships. The victim could be reduced to desperate measures, such as jettisoning its cargo to gain speed, but your prey may just play for time – when night falls, they will stand a better chance of getting away from you under cover of darkness. They might extinguish every light on board and hope that you will sail right past them. Some even set up a light in a little rowing boat to draw you off course. It is a bitter game, and having a good helmsman whom you can trust to act correctly on his own initiative is a great asset.

Show your teeth to your prey

The moment has arrived. You have closed in on your prey, your true colours declaring your dastardly intent. The victim now knows what lies in store for him, so fire a shot across the bows of his ship; he will know what that means, and with any luck he will surrender immediately. If not, you will have to make contact by hailing him. (If there is still no response, then fire again, because clearly this is not a friendly vessel.) What will your target say – what question will you put to him first? You can judge for yourself if the response is likely to be truthful or not. The hail may be hostile right from the start, particularly if both captains are expecting an attack. If you are supremely confident, you could try ordering the ship to lower its topsails – the accepted code for surrender. If not, you will need to find another way to assert your superiority.

Parley: the peaceful alternative

I cannot emphasize enough that you do not always have to fight in order to capture a ship. Your crew is precious, but so is your victim's. If you have thoroughly intimidated your prey by demonstrating during the chase how fierce and determined you are, and they have had a chance to see your fearsome and well-armed crew, then it should be quite straightforward to negotiate a surrender. Their captain will seek to parley – that is, open up a discussion – and if it is agreed you could row over for negotiations. Otherwise, the captain of the ship that you are besieging could be rowed over to your vessel; give them a chance to see how formidable your ship is at close hand.

≫→ Vapouring: a rowdy bunch of drunken pirates can be a frightening sight for an enemy crew, as long as you don't lose the plot and forget your goal.

One way of helping this process along is a little trick known as vapouring: your pirate crew will appear on deck, armed to the teeth, and proceed to get drunk and start behaving in a very threatening, almost crazed manner, dancing and shouting insults at the merchantman's crew. Most pirate ships have a few musicians on board, and nothing shows the great confidence that you have in your victory quite like an entire pirate crew performing a wild war dance on the deck. It never seems to have occurred to any potential victim that this could perhaps be a good moment to mount a counter-attack. Instead, everyone appears so terrified that they are even more susceptible to negotiation than before.

Vapouring is not the only way to speed up a surrender. A certain Jonathan Haroden once came alongside an English ship and demanded that the captain surrender within the next five minutes. He stood beside a cannon with a lighted wick and simply waited until the ship struck her colours, capturing her immediately. Unbeknown to the English, his threat was merely a bluff. Had he fired the cannon, it would have been his one and only shot, because he had no other ammunition on board.

⚓

Attacking a ship

Of course, sometimes negotiations will fail, and then it is time to fight. The pirate captain will prepare the ship for battle, giving the order 'hammocks up and chests down', which means that anything that could possibly get in the way during a fight must be stowed away. The temporary partitions between areas of the ship will be taken down, the decks literally cleared for action ('the deck to be cleared fore and aft!') and the fighting stations equipped ('bring the small arms up to the quarter deck, and every man to his post!'). Every man will indeed know his post: you will have been trained for that during the long days in empty sea. You will stow your hammock in the hold at the bulkheads to provide extra padding against splinters from

cannon fire against the wooden sides. All windows must be shut, or even replaced by doors called 'dead lights' that close them off completely. You may be ordered to help run a length of cloth along the rails to hide the crew from observation, adding to the surprise (if you have not already shown your hand in manic vapouring). Musketeers will bring their weapon chests up to the deck, while carpenters will stand by ready to repair any damage that the ship takes in action; it is essential that the ship's sides are left clear, so that the carpenters can attend to any emergency. They will also take charge of the pumps if the ship is holed. The ship's surgeon (or cook) will be ready to operate on any crew member with a shattered limb.

The setting or stowing of sails is a very important and complicated process that will be directed by the bosun. He will tell you how to sling the sails so that the devices holding them won't easily be shot away – if that were to happen, the sails would drop onto the deck while the fight is taking place. The captain will command the crew to 'set fighting sail', which is an arrangement that allows the ship to be handled by as few men as possible so that the others are

⚓ A pirate ship, hoisting the Jolly Roger, and a British vessel square up to each other.

PAGE 118 The chaos of a sea battle in full swing: great galleons go broadside to broadside and all manner of weaponry is deployed as overboard crew cling to the floating wreckage.

available for the fight. Whatever happens, jump to it! Your life and the lives of all your fellow crewmen will depend on how YOU behave. Pirate assaults tend to unfold in one of three ways:

THE RUNNING FIGHT

Here the two vessels are trying to escape each other, but fighting as they go. One ship will lie just behind the other; if you are being pursued, move as many guns as possible to the stern. Small arms will also be useful in this scenario, particularly if there is a chance of boarding, so keep them about you.

BROADSIDE TO BROADSIDE

The captain of a large merchantman may decide that because his ship's sides are stronger than yours, and can therefore absorb more punishment, he will sit tight, assuming a defensive position and enduring your assault until you run out of steam. It is a war of attrition that might be settled by accident – for example, if either ship's powder magazine is hit and explodes. If the ships are really close to each other, a round shot can easily smash in a plank to a depth of a yard. Such close proximity will also give an advantage to the ship that has the best sharpshooters, whose muskets can clear an enemy deck from aloft in the rigging. Take out the helmsman or the captain, and the ship will be helpless. Bold attackers might also dispatch parties in small boats to get nearer to their target. A determined small boat crew could even wedge the rudder on an enemy ship, so that it would have difficulty turning to avoid a fight. Battles at such close quarters can last for hours, so iron discipline is needed.

THE SEA FIGHT

This is the classic pirate fight, where ships are like two bare-knuckle fighters, each trying to gain the advantage and attack from the best position possible. They will try and try again to manoeuvre their ships into the perfect position for an attack, while their opponent does the same. Here good seamanship is as important as good gunnery. The fight will be thorough, and will probably end with one of the ships being boarded by the other, which we'll come back to later.

PREPARE TO FIGHT

The battleground set, it's time to steel yourself for combat. If you are a ship's gunner, you will find yourself very busy in any of these scenarios. You will be opening the gun ports, ready to roll the cannons out so that their barrels protrude from the ship's side; the ports may have been caulked to keep out the sea, in which case you'll have to give them a good bash. Check your guns carefully. Is there enough grease on the axle-tree? Good lubrication is essential for the cannon to run true. Most important of all, make sure that your charges and gunpowder are dry. You should have ready beside each gun your:

- rammer, with sponge
- handspike and crow
- powder horn and priming wire
- worm and ladle for removing unfired cartridge
- budge barrel (lined with leather) for collecting spilled powder
- linstock (the long pole that will hold your lighted match when ready to fire)

Between every two guns there should be a sponging tub filled with sea water. The cartridges for the guns will be kept elsewhere and brought to the gun, and the matches will be kept amidships (in the middle of the ship floor), one tub for every four guns. Everything thus arranged, you will listen to a final, rousing speech from your captain, who will tell you what a fine crew you are, and remind you that everyone must work together in the battle that is to come. You will all then be given a drink of rum to steady your nerves. A short prayer would also be highly appropriate. As you approach your target – or they approach you! – the

Readying the Cannons

Using your cannons to their maximum devastating potential requires teamwork, and for every member of the crew to know their part. The carrier gives the cartridge to the loader, who forces it as far as possible up the barrel. The rammer rams it home. The shot is then inserted, followed by the wad that will keep it in place. Once the gun has been loaded, you, the gun captain, can commence the firing sequence:

• Remove the tompion. This is the stopper in the cannon's muzzle. It will be left there until the last moment to keep the inside of the barrel as dry as possible.

• Remove the lead apron that covers the touch hole, and pull out the tallowed rope that seals it.

• Prick the cartridge and carefully fill the vent with powder, leaving it heaped. Crush the pile of powder with your powder horn, and then make sure the horn is out of the way. (You may wish to cover the vent again until the moment of ignition.)

• Have the gun crew run the gun out through its port.

• Aim the gun; instruct the gun crew to use their handspikes and crows to adjust it precisely. Crucial to your success will be which part of the enemy ship you decide to aim at. A broadside fired against an enemy's stern can do ten times the damage of one fired against the ship's side, and

means that the enemy can only bring his swivel guns against you.

• Judge when to fire; take heed of the swell of the sea and the relative positions of the two ships.

• Take the linstock (a wooden shaft holding the match at a safe distance), knock it on the match tub to remove any ash and let it fall into the water. Then touch the lighted match to the powder just behind the vent, not on top of it – safety first!

• The cannon will fire, and the recoil will drive it back on board with great violence. Stand well clear!

• Place your thumb over the vent, so that a rush of air does not ignite any powder left behind.

• Have the gun crew clean the barrel out, the loading rammer now using their sponge to swab out the barrel and quench any burning embers left inside.

musicians may well strike up a tune once again, and cheers will go up as the vessels close.

Shots will start to ring out as the battle begins. The first discharges will probably be fired from the ship's cannons, but banish from your mind any hope that a broadside, no matter how fierce it is, is going to sink the enemy ship. A ship may look as though it has been shot to pieces, with

A BREECH-LOADING CANNON

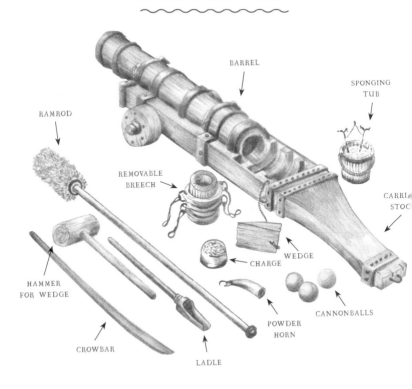

BARREL

SPONGING TUB

RAMROD

REMOVABLE BREECH

CARRIAGE STOCK

HAMMER FOR WEDGE

WEDGE

CHARGE

CANNONBALLS

POWDER HORN

CROWBAR

LADLE

holes in its planking, its masts broken and sails in tatters, but still lumber on. A round shot striking the side of a ship is highly unlikely to produce a hole sufficient to sink a vessel, but it will have devastating effects in other ways. Even if a neat hole is not created, the impact of the cannonball will invariably result in a hail of wood-splinter shrapnel being blown into the ship's interior, onto the unsuspecting gun crew and the other sailors. Would you want to be showered by sharp oak splinters? Such shots delivered against an overcrowded vessel can cripple the ship, putting it out of action not by sinking it – which would result in the loss of treasure anyway – but by disabling its crew.

⚓ This is a fixed-carriage version of a breech-loading variety of cannon, a type that was usually encountered as a swivel gun and mounted in the stern. The breech was secured in place using the hammered wedge.

When the vessels close, muskets, cutlasses and pikes will come into action, with the same aim of incapacitating the crew, not the ship. It will be a horrible sight, and one of the best descriptions of the sheer awfulness of it comes from a man called Pantero Pantera, who fought on Mediterranean galleys and wrote of:

> *the havoc wrought among human limbs now by iron now by fire (which is not so terrifying in land battles), the sight of this man torn to shreds and in the same moment another burned up, another drowned, another pierced by an arquebus ball, yet another split into wretched pieces by the artillery. On top of this there is the terror caused by the sight of a vessel swallowed up by the sea with all hands without the remotest possibility of rescue, to see the crew half alive, half burned, sink miserably to the bottom while the sea changes colour and turns red with human blood, covered the while with arms and scraps and fragments of broken ships.*

It's not just the enemy you have to fear; men can also be very badly burned by the flames from their own guns, or by cartridges exploding accidentally. Whatever the cause, the sheer sight of numerous dead bodies will demoralize your crew, so corpses should be concealed from view, even though they may also frighten the enemy. This may not always be possible in the heat of battle, however; shattered limbs and torsos are the invariable result of cannon fire, so stiffen your resolve.

Boarding techniques

By the time boarding takes place, it is likely that both crews will have prepared for the action, unless of course the pirate crew have until now kept themselves hidden from view, disguised as a friendly vessel and boarding only at the very last minute, with no preliminary bombardment.

←« Pirates haul themselves up the side of a Spanish galleon, with weapons out, ready to fight. This is a very difficult operation, because you will be climbing from an unstable boat and your attackers have the advantage of height.

»→ A band of British privateers meet their victims in hand-to-hand combat; note the typical use of the pistol as a club by the fellow at bottom right.

Otherwise, the attackers' intentions will be fairly obvious, even through the din of cannon fire and the obscuring smoke, and manoeuvering for position takes time. The choice of boarding position is crucial. Alongside or amidships is best. Boarding at the stern is not advised, because that is where swivel guns may be mounted, and there is a greater height to climb. Perhaps the captain has chosen to launch a night attack, capitalizing on the element of surprise – but the confusion can be as great for the attacker as for the attacked. In order to secure a passage to the other ship, grappling hooks fitted with long ropes will be made ready, and if your helmsman is really skilled, he can steer the ship so that your bowsprit (the mast that sticks out forwards from the bows) provides a useful boarding platform.

In a large crew, there will usually be a dedicated boarding party. It is not easy jumping from one ship to another, because the two vessels may rock up and down violently, and some boarding opportunities may be missed when the ships suddenly part company, tearing and splitting ropes in two and even leaving boarders stranded on the enemy deck. The risks can be great, but you may wish to put yourself forward as a first boarder – they are often richly rewarded, and given their choice of weapon from the defeated crew. This is quite a bonus on top of your share of the spoils – that is, if you live that long. Now is the time to take up your pistols and cutlasses, and perhaps also an axe, or even exploding grenades, for smashing down defences. Others in your party may have muskets or blunderbusses, and some specialized equipment will be needed, such as wedges to keep the enemy gun ports tightly shut and spikes to block the touch holes of the enemy cannons, rendering them useless.

Once aboard, your captain will have to make a decision about where to attack, depending on where the enemy crew are likely to be located. They may have retreated down below and locked themselves away, or they may have resolved to stay up on deck and fight you. In the latter case, as much fire as possible should be poured down onto the decks and into

the rigging, to clear them of men before your boarding party takes over. There will be a lot of smoke, but your musketeers must seek out the dangers through the fog and deal with them. As

»» A crew under pirate attack may desperately scramble below decks and attempt to wait the fight out from the relative safety of the ship's hull.

for you, with your cutlass, you must cut through any nets or cloths placed there to hinder your progress before you get to grips with an enemy sailor.

If the enemy have taken cover below, they can easily counter-attack, as the French privateer Jean Doublet discovered when attacking an English ship. He had used grenades to clear the decks, but a blunderbuss was suddenly fired at him from a loophole. The shot missed, but a door then opened, and more shots were fired, followed by a cutlass attack. Somehow, despite this sneaky assault, he survived!

A ship about to be boarded may be so well prepared that she has time to deliver one last broadside at point-blank range, and as her crew run to safety they will let off explosions on the deck to catch the boarders. Though a besieged captain will not always prioritize the safety of their crew; I recall the tale of the Comte de Forbin, who was attacked by a Dutch privateer. Instead of ordering his men to the safety of closed quarters, the privateer captain secured his hatches from the outside, so that none of his men could retreat or hide; they had no choice but to fight to the death.

Whatever the ploy, the outcome will be bloody. You will discharge your pistols, and then seize your cutlass (there will be no time for reloading). Watch your step, because the enemy may have spread dried peas on the deck to make you slip, or scattered about caltrops – nasty iron twists of spikes, that always fall with one spike upwards. Tread on one of those and you will be slowed down so rapidly that someone will easily pick you off as a sitting target.

It will then be a hand-to-hand fight, and nothing I can say will ade-quately prepare you for the combat. Just think of what it will leave behind: severed limbs, concussed skulls, horrific wounds made by cuts and bullets. The surgeon will do his best, but if a limb is broken the only recourse is to amputate it – hence the old sailors you see walking around with wooden

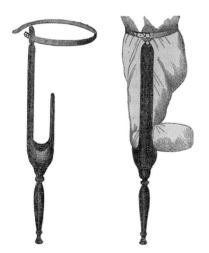

←≪ Everyone imagines pirates with wooden legs (and eye patches!), but wounded men died during the amputation, so someone with a wooden leg must be regarded as relatively fortunate.

≫→ The head of Blackbeard, hanging from the bow of Lieutenant Robert Maynard's ship, the HMS *Pearl*, as proof of his victory (and thus eligibility for his bounty).

legs. On top of the loss of life, there may even be a loss of treasure; the ship's cargo may be burned by accident, or may even be deliberately thrown into the sea by a captain determined to thwart your dastardly efforts. You can see why most pirate captains prefer to negotiate...

Let me conclude by reminding you of one of the most famous battles on the deck of a pirate ship. The ship was the sloop *Adventure*, commanded by Blackbeard. On 22 November 1718, *Adventure* was taken by surprise off Ocracoke Island, North Carolina, by two vessels carrying over sixty men under the command of Lieutenant Robert Maynard of the Royal Navy. Blackbeard cut his anchor cable and tried to flee, but being unable to do so on that windless morning his crew bravely took the fight to the enemy. They swept the decks with fire and thought that the naval ships had been largely disabled, but when Blackbeard's men boarded, they found themselves the victims of an ambush, as the sailors reappeared from the cabins below decks where they had sheltered from the initial cannon fire. That gave them the victory against the notorious pirate captain, and they hung his head from the bowsprit of their ship, proclaiming their success (and effectively warning off any other would-be attackers).

Plunder and prisoners

Assuming that there is some treasure left on board, any pirate worthy of the name will loot his prey. An East India Company ship will yield rich spoils: spices, gold and cloth. There is also likely to be a money chest, along with charts, maps and navigational instruments. Good maps and charts are highly prized. Very important too are the rutters – the logs of a voyage, showing dangerous places. When Bartholomew Sharpe captured a Spanish ship in 1681, the crew tried to throw their logbook overboard. Sharpe retrieved it, noting how the Spanish cried when they saw him get hold of it, because they knew that it would help him make fresh conquests based on the information it contained.

New sails packed away below decks can be very welcome, not to mention food and drink. Buoyed up by victory, the successful pirate crew will probably drink whatever is on board there and then, unless the captain forbids it until they are safely away from any additional danger – the guard ships of a convoy, for instance. Captured cargo, such as sugar and slaves, has to be sold on to raise a profit, but for that to happen the captain needs to find a friendly port. Thus the notion of a 'pirate haven' developed; a place where goods could be sold or exchanged without interference from the authorities or questions being asked. New Providence was one, until it was forced to close after a naval raid in 1718. If selling the cargo seems impossible, then a victorious pirate crew may ignore everything except for food, drink and money, indulging in a little pillaging and then throwing everything else overboard.

There are strict rules governing a privateer's looting. As privateers work for a government or company, then (theoretically at least) everything

⚓ Sir Francis Drake's pocket-book. Such logs divulged otherwise inaccessible information about weather patterns and trading routes that any pirate worth his salt could exploit for his own personal gain.

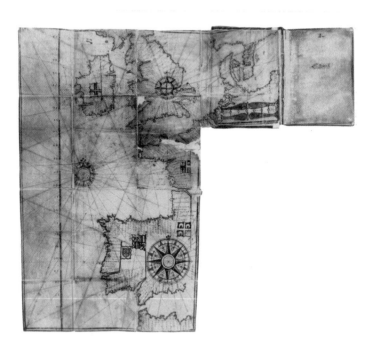

has to be handed over to their sponsor – but there is usually some leeway granted, so that a privateer may keep some of what he seizes. Sometimes this is written into their Letter of Marque, and may be expressed as a percentage of the total spoils. Plunder books will be kept by the ship's quartermaster, listing what has been taken. Among pirates (real pirates!), however, there is no such requirement, over and above that which the captain will already have decided is fair shares for the crew.

The biggest prize of all is the ship you have captured – so what should you do with it? The easiest course is to strip it of anything valuable and then set fire to it. However, perhaps someone might wish to buy it. Otherwise, it could be ransomed back to its original owners, though negotiations can be a little difficult after you have stolen someone's ship! Of course, you could keep it for yourself, adding it to your pirate fleet or even adopting it as your main ship if it is a particularly fine vessel. Your own ship will no doubt have taken some damage in the fray and need to be repaired. It could be in a dreadful mess, so put into a safe harbour and get to work.

Finally, whether you have taken a ship by force or through peaceful surrender, you are likely to have a large number of prisoners on your hands. They should be secured as soon as possible, and certainly before your victorious crew begins the celebrations. Put them in the hold and shackle them. It may not be pleasant, but it will prevent them from mounting a rebellion – one in which you may find yourself outnumbered. There are stories of brave sailors who have escaped their chains and taken over their floating prison. Don't let it happen to you.

6

Land Ho!
The Pirate Raid

Piracy on dry land

Ship-to-ship fighting is not the be all and end all of a pirate's life; land is where the money lies. During the Golden Age of Piracy, Spain minted coins in silver and gold, and these became our favoured shared currency. Silver coins (*reales*) and gold coins (*escudos*) each come in various denominations, the famous 'Piece of Eight' being the largest of the silver coins, with a distinctive '8' stamped into it, weighing approximately one ounce. You may also have heard of a 'doubloon', a name coming from the Spanish *doblón*, which means to double; thus a doubloon is a coin of double value. Such tender flows freely in the trading ports along the Spanish Main, and so if they are serious about plunder, and have the opportunity to sell it afterwards, your captain may lead you on a raid against a coastal town.

Jean L'Olonnais, a buccaneer who terrorized the Caribbean in the 1600s, was one of the most successful pirates who ever carried out land attacks. So daring was he that he would often attack with only a comparatively small force of men. Amongst the most lucrative of these short and sharp raids of his was an assault on the town of Maracaibo, Venezuela, where he seized thousands of Spanish dollars. Legends (probably exaggerated) tell vividly of his savage tactics: that he would hack his victims to pieces bit by bit, or squeeze a cord around their necks until their eyes popped out – rumours that L'Olonnais encouraged, because they made his reputation all the more terrifying. Ironic, then, that he is said to have met his fate when he was captured and eaten

↑ A gold doubloon – real pirate treasure!

by cannibals. Perhaps best not to tempt karma with excessive cruelty.

By contrast, during the fourteenth and fifteenth centuries, huge *wako* raids against Chinese and Korean towns were mounted by fleets so large that they were effectively armies. Some treacherous Chinese people worked for the *wako* as guides and informants, hoping for a share of the pirates' spoils. (They could also be coerced into doing this to avoid being killed, of course, but many were willing accomplices.) Quite often the object of the *wako* raids was to capture slaves. Captured artisans were generally well treated and rewarded for their labour, so that they would make weapons for pirates engaged in an extended raid, but captives could also be put to horrible use to aid in the pirates' tactics. Prisoners might be dressed up to look like pirates and made to carry out attacks at the head of the real pirate army, their tongues cut out so that they could not betray the plot. As a result of this practice, many innocent captives were executed by the Chinese, while genuine pirates were released. The pirates also forced women to attack Chinese troops, or drive herds of sheep before them to cover their approach. As an alternative way of drawing the enemy fire one or two pirates might make a suicide attack.

A typical *wako* raid would be carried out by a fleet of ships, each about thirty strong, sailing no more than 100 to 200 yards apart from each other. They communicated by using conch-shell trumpets, so that one section could aid another in distress, and advanced like a long slithering snake. Particularly fierce warriors were deployed at the front and rear of a squad. When facing a Chinese army, the *wako* leader would wave his fan and his followers would brandish their swords; this created an effect that has been described as looking like a swarm of butterflies. While the Chinese army watched anxiously, the pirates would rush into the attack, and would storm an encampment slashing furiously with their swords. But there was method in the madness; they would avoid walls from which stones might be dropped on them, and stay out of alleyways and narrow streets in case of ambush, and even make captives taste any food or drink in case it was poisoned. Before setting fires in towns, the *wako* would cover their own ships in wet bedding for protection.

The Japanese were also cunning strategists in combat. In a fierce series of *wako* raids mounted against the Spanish colonists in the Philippines between 1581 and 1586, the Japanese pirates would fearlessly charge forward, waving their swords, terrifying their victims into retreat and defeat; but eventually the Spaniards realized they could fire volleys of bullets and cannonballs at the oncoming waves of men from within the protection of their fortifications. Another death-defying Japanese tactic was one that the *wako* learned to employ against Spanish pikemen. It was a technique never encountered in Europe or South America, whereby the Japanese recipient of a pike-thrust ignored the wound it had inflicted and instead turned the assault to his own advantage, seizing the pike that had cut or even impaled him and using it to drag the pikeman off his feet. The man could then be finished off with a swift sword stroke. But in 1581, one clever Spanish captain had the pikes greased on the upper half, in order that his men might be able to draw them from the bodies and the hands of the Japanese pirates; this manoeuvre turned the tables in the following conflicts. By a combination of tricks like this, together with the increased use of fortifications and intense cannon fire, the *wako* threat was controlled.

☠

The successful pirate raid and how to achieve it

You will equip your raiding party very similarly to the ship's boarding party, issuing your crew with cutlasses, pistols or axes. The big difference will be that you will also have to carry provisions and water with you. It is unlikely that your band of raiders will drag cannons ashore, unless you need to smash down walls or gates, because they will slow your movements and lose you the element of surprise; pistols and muskets will be your firearms of choice.

First you will drop anchor in the bay. Having left guards on the ship, you will put ashore in small boats, perhaps rowing a long way upriver

⚑ The English privateer Thomas Cavendish facing attack from the natives upon making landfall in South America – perhaps they objected to the invaders' destruction of wildlife.

– some of the best targets lie further inland. You must expect to get very wet, but cartridges need to be kept dry, of course. Once you have reached your target, you will leave your boats on the seashore or the river bank, and don't forget to mount a guard in case you have to retreat; though some very bold pirates burn their boats to show that they have no intentions of retreating. Often a pirate raiding band will hide among the mangroves until daybreak, and then attack, although a night attack could be the best bet if there are sentries posted.

Then it is time to move en masse against your target, just like the Japanese *wako*. This will be easy if you have targeted a port town with a good landing area; otherwise, you may have a distance to travel, crossing rivers and cutting through jungle. The further from water a town is, the greater the likelihood of you being spotted. Ideally, your target will not be too far from your landing point; a long march gives the weather opportunity to turn against you, and if you do experience sudden and heavy rain, your guns may be rendered useless, giving the town's garrison, who have been able to shelter, a significant advantage. Further, over a very long march your units may get separated, so make sure that each carries a flag, so that your comrades can recognize each other; an extended journey also gives certain undesirables within your party the chance to wander off on a little raid of their own. Such stragglers must not be tolerated. Punish them severely.

If your presence is revealed while on the march, the town's defenders may try to ambush you – if they are brave enough to risk it. Avoid this by taking a less obvious route to your target. Local guides will be very useful in this regard, so if you encounter an enemy sentry, do not simply kill him – he could be a valuable source of information. The story of a group of Javanese pirates who attacked Ayutthaya, the old capital of Siam, in about 1623 demonstrates the downside of being noticed before you are close enough to mount your attack. The King of Siam had previously imprisoned eight Japanese soldiers for their part in a rebellion, and promised the captives their liberty if they would help rid his

↟ Pirates operating on land are shown taking over a city in this original painting by Howard Pyle in his *Book of Pirates*.

country of the invaders. The soldiers acted decisively, proposing that as many Siamese troops as possible should be equipped with Japanese armour and helmets, the sight of which would surely terrify the attackers. Seventy suits of armour were found, and eight war elephants were made available. The eight Japanese samurai took command of the disguised company, together with an additional 500 Siamese soldiers, and placed two small cannons on each elephant's back. This army set out for the coast, and as soon as they came in sight of the Javanese ships, they began a furious cannonade, which would speedily have sunk the whole fleet, had the pirates not prudently retreated.

I do not expect that you will have cannons fired at you from elephants, but take care at all times, and as you draw close to your objective it may be a good idea to send on ahead a 'forlorn hope' party who can probe the enemy's defences, revealing their strengths and weaknesses. If the town is weakly defended, you would be wise to storm the place straight away; wait for dawn only if you have marched all night and your crew is in need of a rest. Study the fortifications that you will need to overcome. They may range from bags of sand to quite formidable stone walls, such as those at Cartagena or Panama. Grenades will be useful during the assault, and make sure that your musketeers target any artillerymen – cannons cannot fire at you on their own! There will also be huge dangers once you break through the defences. Desperate defenders will hide round each and every corner to ambush you, so never drop your guard.

Once you have captured the settlement, it needs to be secured; do not let your men start plundering so enthusiastically that this is forgotten. In Spain, the best place to secure the town is the church – it's a good idea to go inside and give thanks to God for the prize he has given you, because the Spanish are unlikely to mount a counter-attack if it means harming their church. Place sentries up in the tower, from where they will have a good view of any potential assailants. Pillage and plunder can then take place in relative safety, but if this is the only motivation for taking the town then make sure that it is done as quickly as possible, before reinforcements arrive.

Great pirate raids

You should always seek out examples to follow when you are planning your pirate activities. Let others take the risks, and learn from their successes – and failures. Here are some of the most famous land raids in pirate history.

ZHEJIANG 1556

One of the greatest raids ever committed in the Far East was master-minded by two Chinese pirates called Xu Hai and Wang Zhi, who launched a massive campaign against China's Zhejiang province in the spring and summer of 1556. Several thousand *wako* sailed from Japan and landed near the mouth of the Yangtze River, while others threatened Shanghai, but these operations were merely diversionary tactics to mask their real target – the fortified city of Dongxiang. The main raiding party destroyed their own boats upon landing – a bold declaration that they were not going to withdraw.

They were opposed by a Chinese leader called Hu Dongxian, who used cunning to overcome his rivals' military superiority – he thwarted one group of raiders simply by loading a boat with poisoned wine. The *wako*, predictably, made merry with the wine, with fatal consequences. But Xu Hai's main army arrived at the walled city of Dongxiang nevertheless, laying siege to it using a wide range of sophisticated weaponry: cannons, assault towers mounted on boats and a giant battering ram suspended in a transportable framework. The newly built city wall nevertheless held out

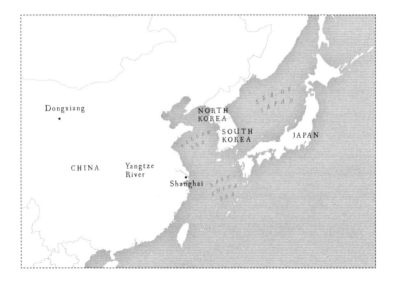

↟ The region in which *wako* pirates operated.

well against the fierce assault. The *wako* decided to starve the garrison into submission, but the city was well prepared, and the frustrated pirates eventually abandoned the attempt after five miserable months.

The siege of Dongxiang averted, Hu Dongxian reasoned that the *wako*'s main concern now was how to get back to Japan with the booty they had captured elsewhere. Having burned their own boats on arrival, they loaded their loot onto captured Chinese vessels, which formed a long and

vulnerable crocodile. Hu Dongxian made them an offer: those wishing to surrender would be employed within the Chinese military, while those wishing to return to Japan would be supplied with vessels to allow them to do so. It was a bold gamble. He knew that there had been some disagreement among the *wako* leaders about what to do next, and watched while they fell out with each other. Rival *wako* commanders turned against their erstwhile leader, and an internal battle began. Eventually, weary from their long campaign and weakened by their in-fighting, the *wako* army destroyed itself.

PANAMA, 1671

One of the most famous pirate raids in history was launched against the Spanish colony on Panama in 1671 by Henry Morgan. Having led successful raids in the area over the past decade, he decided that an operation on a much more ambitious scale was in order. When the news spread around the pirate communities that none other than Captain Morgan, by then a renowned hero, was sailing once again for the Spanish Main, hundreds of pirates sailed to his Caribbean refuge – an isolated island near Hispaniola – to join him and prepare the attack. Morgan set his sights on Panama

◂◂◂ Attempts by the Chinese authorities to tackle piracy in the South China Sea.

⚓ The entrance to the Chagres River, Panama, overlooked by Fort San Lorenzo.

City, a bold choice: as the city lay on the Pacific side of the Isthmus of Panama, the thin strip of land between the Caribbean Sea and the Pacific Ocean, the privateers would have to go overland. The best route was along the Chagres River and then through dense jungle, but first they would have to overcome Fort San Lorenzo at the mouth of the river. Speed was essential; the Spanish were aware of the large buccaneer force massing in the Caribbean, and they wouldn't hesitate to send reinforcements to the likely targets. And so Colonel Bradley, one of Morgan's leading officers, hurried to Fort San Lorenzo. His 470 men in three ships would not stand a chance against the fort's gunfire, so he launched a land assault, marching against the fort on 6 January 1671. In spite of heavy enemy fire, the men managed to get close enough to lob firebombs and grenades into the fort – a wooden structure that had a thatched roof in places, which eventually caught fire. Many of the defenders snuck out under cover of darkness, and when the buccaneers attacked again at dawn the last defenders were killed and the fort surrendered. It was a fierce fight, with heavy losses on both sides; Bradley himself was among the hundred or so privateers who died in

the assault. Henry Morgan landed a few days later, and his hundreds of men repaired the fortress as quickly as they could. Leaving 300 men as a garrison, the main force of seven small ships and thirty-six boats and canoes paddled up the river as far as they could go, and on 19 January they set off into the jungle by foot, bristling with weapons. On 28 January 1671 the buccaneers finally arrived at the gates of Panama. Though the forces were fairly well matched in size, Morgan's men had better weapons and more experience – cavalry were the defenders' only real advantage, though they also had a secret weapon in the shape of oxen that they planned to stampede. Morgan attacked early on the morning of 28 January and took a small hill, giving him an advantage over Don Juan's advancing army – the Spanish cavalry were simply picked off by French sharpshooters.

The Spanish infantry then moved forward in a disorganized charge, to which Morgan responded with an effective counter-attack. The inexperienced Spanish soon fell into a disorderly retreat, the oxen trick having failed. Five hundred

⚑ Map of Panama, showing key points along Morgan's route.

↟ Captain Morgan's band of privateers stayed in Panama for about four weeks after their raid, digging through the ashes to ensure they had extracted all the loot they could.

Spaniards were killed for only fifteen buccaneers. The pirates chased the survivors back into the city, and there was chaos in the streets as the retreating Spaniards tried to burn as much of the city as they could. Several Spanish ships managed to flee under the cover of the smoke with the bulk of the city's wealth by the time Morgan secured it. But the raid was not rendered fruitless – over the next four weeks, the buccaneers determinedly pursued Spanish fugitives in the hills and looted the small islands in the bay where so many had tried to conceal their treasures. The haul was so large that it took 175 mules to carry the treasure back to the Atlantic coast, along with numerous Spanish prisoners for ransom.

VERACRUZ, 1683

In 1683, a raid took place against the port of Veracruz in New Spain, Mexico – in fact, a target that Henry Morgan had considered before settling on Panama City in 1671. On 17 May pirates under the Dutch Captain Van Hoorn arrived off the coast of Veracruz with a small fleet of five large vessels, eight smaller vessels and over 1,000 pirates. Two captured

Spanish ships headed the fleet, a stratagem it was hoped would lead the townsfolk to believe that the fleet was a friendly Spanish convoy.

»→ Captain Henry Morgan overseeing the sack of Panama in 1671.

A raiding party was sent ahead, and early the following morning, while most of the town's militia was sleeping, the raiders disabled the town's fortifications, enabling a larger force of pirates to enter the city. They sacked the town and took a large number of hostages, including the town's governor. But the next day, as a Spanish war fleet loomed on the horizon, the pirates retreated to a nearby island, taking their hostages to wait for ransom payments. But these payments did not arrive immediately, and there was some debate about what to do. Most of the pirates wanted to give the Spaniards more time, but their impatient leaders ordered the execution of a dozen prisoners and had their heads sent to Veracruz as a warning. Even so, the Spanish were not to be moved. Eventually the pirates gave up and moved on with their booty, leaving the surviving hostages to their fate.

As you can see, raiding ashore is by no means a simple alternative to fighting on the high seas. Land raids are military operations that only work if they are planned well, and backed up with significant resources. A raid by a small force can go disastrously wrong. Henry Morgan and the *wako* chiefs of Japan may have had the authority to command these armies, but most pirate captains will not have charge of such considerable firepower. That is, nevertheless, an ideal to which you should aspire; read on, to find out how you may join the ranks of the greatest pirate captains.

7

The Successful Pirate Captain

Don't be surprised by the inclusion of this chapter, my friend! I do not expect that recruits with your training will remain crewmen all their lives. I think you have captain potential.

Pirate management
The good captain's guide to human resources

When you are elected to the rank of captain, it is most advisable to draw up a Pirates' Code that will govern your ship. This will set out what you require from your crew with no ambiguity or misunderstanding. John Phillips, captain of the *Revenge*, set out the following guidelines in 1724:

I. Every Man Shall obey civil Command; the Captain shall have one full Share and a half of all Prizes; the Master, Carpenter, Boatswain and Gunner shall have one Share and quarter. (*Note that you get nothing!*)

II. If any Man shall offer to run away, or keep any Secret from the Company, he shall be marooned with one Bottle of Powder, one Bottle of Water, one small Arm, and Shot. (*No food of course — perhaps the bullet will be used on himself..?*)

III. If any Man shall steal any Thing in the Company, or game, to the Value of a Piece of Eight, he shall be marooned or shot. (*It's not worth it!*)

IV. If any time we shall meet another Marooner that Man shall sign his Articles without the Consent of our Company, shall suffer such Punishment as the Captain and Company shall think fit. (*This means that pirates stick together and obey their own captain. No desertions either!*)

V. That Man that shall strike another whilst these Articles are in force, shall receive Moses' Law (that is, 40 Stripes lacking one) on the bare Back. (*The idea comes from the Bible, and is painful!*)

VI. That Man that shall snap his Arms, or smoke Tobacco in the Hold, without a Cap to his Pipe, or carry a Candle lighted without a Lantern, shall suffer the same Punishment as in the former Article. (*You now understand my warnings about the dangers of fire on board — it is not something to be taken lightly.*)

VII. That Man shall not keep his Arms clean, fit for an Engagement, or neglect his Business, shall be cut off from his Share, and suffer such other Punishment as the Captain and the Company shall think fit. (*If your pistol isn't clean it won't work, and what use will you be to your crewmates in battle then?*)

VIII. If any Man shall lose a Joint in time of an Engagement, shall have 400 Pieces of Eight; if a Limb, 800. (*It sounds generous but it is small recompense for you losing your pirate career.*)

IX. If at any time you meet with a prudent Woman, that Man that offers to meddle with her, without her Consent, shall suffer present Death. (*Women are to be respected at all times!*)

←≪ Howard Pyle's portrait of the perfect pirate captain. He carries a musket and has a pistol at his belt, but it is his air of authority that is most intimidating.

≫→ This illustration from Charles Ellm's *The Pirate's Own Book* shows a woman from a pirate crew in the midst of a chaotic land raid.

You will need to prepare something along these lines, but bear in mind that in addition to drawing up the Code you must also live by it yourself; it is essential that you set a good example to your crew, and particularly important that you are not seen to be hypocritical, which is sure to breed resentment and may even lead to mutiny. Black Bart is a fine role model to follow. He was always smartly dressed, he never touched alcohol, he never swore and he kept the Sabbath day holy.

Punishment and discipline

As a captain, you will be the master of experienced seamen. I have nothing but contempt for those landlubbers who end up on a ship convinced that as pirates they are nothing more than soldiers who happen to have ended up on the sea. They won't last long under sail, I can tell you. Theirs will be

Women on board

You'll notice that the Pirates' Code repeated here specifically refers to every 'Man' on board the ship – but what about women? The Articles of Agreement covering conduct on board pirate ships often included strict prohibitions on having women aboard, one set of regulations going so far as to

state that 'Women are weak, feckless, hysterical beings who distract men and bring bad luck to ships, calling forth supernatural winds that sink vessels and drown men'. But historical records prove that women did, and do, go to sea as pirates or sailors – though often they had to hide their true identity. A woman wishing to become a pirate may need to embrace the mannerisms common to the men of the ship – fighting, swearing and over-indulging – to fit in. The disguise itself is not difficult to pull off; pirates wear their hair long, tied in a pigtail and tarred, and if a crew member doesn't shave, the other men will simply assume he hasn't gone through puberty. And the petticoat breeches and baggy shirt worn by sailors can easily hide a woman's shape. After all, sailors rarely remove their clothes; the only time a doctor insists they undress is to treat their wounds. Take the case of Billy Bridle, a daring sailor of two years' standing. After challenging a shipmate to climb the highest mast, Billy followed, but on the descent lost his grip, fell to the deck and died. It was only during the inquest that Billy was discovered to be a girl called Rachel Young.

Women are tough, so furling and unfurling sails, working the pumps, rowing boats, and a myriad of other on-board tasks requiring hard labour will not be a problem for most women; ashore they work equally long hours and do physically demanding chores. If she is strong and willing, a woman is more than capable of doing a pirate's work. And she may have an understanding crew – remember the cases of Anne Bonny, Mary Read and Rachel Wall, all of whom earned their place on board without pretence.

the ships that run aground or strike reefs. This is where discipline comes in – though the discipline on board a pirate ship is often very lax compared to what you would expect on a merchantman or man-of-war.

Good discipline starts with the captain, although some captains confuse punishment with discipline and hand out unjust punishments for minor breaches of conduct. Far better to set out clearly what is expected of your crew with a Pirates' Code, and then properly enforce it. The quartermaster will punish pirates on your behalf for minor infractions, such as quarrelling, abusing prisoners, and failing to keep weapons clean. The most severe offences, including murdering a fellow pirate, disobeying orders during battle, or deserting the ship, will be your responsibility to deal with. While the quartermaster will immediately shoot any deserters who are caught, a trial should be held in all other circumstances, and those found guilty will receive whatever sentence the crew deems fair. But what kind of punishments can you expect to witness – I hope not endure – during your pirate career?

Keelhauling is a most brutal and sadistic punishment that all but guarantees death, as the wrongdoer is half-drowned and raked over by the barnacles on your ship's hull.

A chained prisoner is branded by the authorities. Such punishment is especially cruel, since the convict is forevermore marked with his crime.

BRANDING

This is not one for your crew, but all pirates should be aware that they risk this severe punishment. It is used by the authorities, because branding with a red-hot iron is the most secure way of identifying a pirate in case of future misdemeanours. The East India Company brands the forehead of every pirate they catch with the letter 'P'. For a captain to so afflict one of his men would be a very serious breach of pirate conduct, because the man's life would then be in danger wherever he went.

KEELHAULING

Keelhauling is a most unpleasant and serious punishment. A rope is passed under the belly of the ship by divers. Once it is in place, the felon is tied to one end of it and thrown overboard. Crewmen then pull the other end to drag him underwater. You can first bind the criminal's wrists and hoist him out to the main yard with a weighted line attached to his feet, stretching him out quite painfully, if you wish to prolong the experience. One of your crew will then cover the guilty man's face with an

← Walking the plank is probably the best-known of all pirate punishments, although it is unlikely that it ever really happened during the Golden Age of Piracy. Nevertheless, Howard Pyle included it in his book in dramatic fashion, with the unfortunate victim both tied up and blindfolded.

↓ A wrongdoer might be tarred and feathered, a punishment designed for humiliation.

oily rag to prevent him from drowning, then he is dropped into the sea and the line hauled in, dragging him under the water against the ship's hull where barnacles slash his skin before he resurfaces on the opposite side. It is traditionally done three times, so very few survive the ordeal. Towing, a simpler variation of keelhauling, involves tying the accused to a line fastened to the stern. As the ship continues its voyage the man is dragged through the ocean, left to die of hypothermia and exhaustion in cold waters, and to the mercy of sharks in warmer climes...

WALKING THE PLANK

I am sure you have heard of this practice, although I can think of no definite instances when it ever has been done. It is traditionally associated with captured prisoners, not guilty crew, so I suspect it has been fabricated by a crafty pirate hoping to make our reputation even more fearsome. The

← Pirates can expect to find themselves flogged by either their captains or the official authorities if they are caught violating either's laws. Flogging is only the beginning of much suffering for the pirate who is unfortunate enough to get caught.

tales tell that a prisoner is tormented by being made to walk out on a plank over the ocean, with a sword to help him on his way, until he topples over the edge. You could try it – be a pioneer!

TARRING AND FEATHERING

This punishment involves humiliation rather than pain. The felon is rolled in tar and then has feathers thrown at him until he resembles an overlarge seagull. He will look ridiculous and feel ashamed, and it will be a long time before his mates let him forget the ordeal. Such humiliation makes for a good deterrent, for both the punished man and the witnesses.

FLOGGING

The punishment most commonly inflicted on pirates is flogging, using a special whip known as the 'cat o' nine tails'. The nine thick strands of a rope are unwound, knotted and covered with tar. For maximum grisly effect, tie fish-hooks or metal balls to the ends of each. The man to be flogged has his shirt removed before being tied to a cannon to endure his forty lashes. You might add 'pickling' to the flogging – pouring salt water or vinegar over the wounds. This punishment is also used by the admirals of Great Britain's Royal Navy, and the judiciary.

Marooning

All of these sentences pale, however, in comparison to the most dreaded punishment of all: marooning. Only the most heinous crimes are rewarded thus – stealing from the crew, abandoning one's post in battle, or inciting mutiny (unsuccessfully). It is the cruellest form of torment for a pirate to become 'Governor of the Island', and I am sure you have heard of the practice, which has become as famous as the idea of a pirate itself. By contrast to the swift, painful end that pirates who undergo keelhauling meet, marooning promises a long, slow death. Normally a prisoner or a mutineer will simply be left on his own to die on an uninhabited island, although it can also happen to a captain whose rebellious crew has taken over the ship. Edward England suffered a mutiny on board ship and was marooned by his crew on the island of Mauritius, along with two loyal men.

Just think how it feels as you watch the ship sail away. Marooning usually meant certain death, the islands being deliberately chosen because of their lack of resources, even to the extent that some captains would select sand bars that would be covered by the tide within a few hours. You will recall that Captain John Phillips' Pirates' Code specified that a marooned man should be left with one bottle of powder, a bottle of water, a small arm and shot. The pistol and its single bullet, of course, were intended to compel the man to commit suicide, succumbing to the hopelessness of his situation. He could attempt to hunt for food, but what if there was no fresh water? Worst of all, a marooned pirate who managed to attract the attention of a passing ship could not even automatically assume he would be picked up and saved, for the crew would suspect that he had broken the Pirates' Code and would be unlikely to want him on board.

Despite all this, on rare occasions, marooned pirates have survived. You may have heard of a sailor called Alexander Selkirk, who was marooned on an island 400 miles west of Chile. Fortunately for

him, the island had plentiful wildlife including goats, whose meat supplied his diet and whose skins became his clothes – in fact, he grew so content in his island haven that when he was found, he was somewhat reluctant to leave. The same is not true of a man called Phillip Ashton.

⚑ Andrew Selkirk, stranded but content on his remote island.

≫→ One of Ned Low's crew shooting a wounded Spaniard; Low had a reputation for cruelty, shared by some of his men.

He was a nineteen-year-old fisherman from Marblehead, Massachusetts, who was captured in the fishing grounds of Nova Scotia in June 1722 by pirates led by Ned Low. Low persuaded some of the fishermen to join his crew and become pirates, but Ashton refused, recording later that he was beaten, whipped, kept in chains and threatened with death many times. He was taken to the West Indies and when allowed to go for water on the island of Roatán, off the coast of Honduras, he took his opportunity to flee the pirate guard. The ship abandoned him, so Ashton was effectively marooned – if voluntarily. Fortunately, there was enough life on the island to sustain him – he survived mainly on crabs, fish, and seabird eggs. He remained there for six months until the brig *Diamond* of Salem under Captain Dove happened to stop there for water and rescued him. Ashton arrived safely home in May 1725.

Similarly, when mutineers seized Captain William Greenaway's ship, they marooned him for refusing to join their pirate ranks. At first, the pirates landed him and seven others on an uninhabited island in the Bahamas without food, water or clothing, but the pirates appear to have suffered guilty feelings and returned later to transfer the victims to a captured sloop anchored a mile from shore – though they cannot have felt too guilty, for again they were abandoned without food. Hope seemed lost, but Greenaway swam ashore, built a raft and returned with

food. Again the pirates couldn't stay away – returning to find that the men had repaired the sloop's sails and rigging, they sank the ship and returned the men to the island. Eight days later, the pirates came back once more, and forced Greenaway and two others to join them. The pirates returned twice more; the first time to deposit supplies, and the second to burn the shelter built by the remaining marooned crew. Not long after, Spaniards captured the pirates, and on hearing about the stranded men they carried out a rescue.

◆

Mutiny – every captain's nightmare

Of course, as you are doling out punishments, you must bear in mind that as captain you run the risk of suffering the greatest punishment of all – mutiny. There is no greater challenge to a captain's authority: the ultimate act of rebellion by a crew eager to oust their captain and seize the ship for themselves. A mutiny is the ultimate betrayal of trust, but do not judge the crew before hearing their case – there are, of course, occasions on which mutiny is deserved, when cruel or ineffective captains have mis-treated their men. Take the case of Ned Low, a Boston ship rigger turned pirate captain, and an exceptionally cruel one, described as a maniac and a brute even by his own crew. He once made the commander of a captured Nantucket whaler eat his own sliced-off ears, sprinkled with salt, before killing him, and when he captured the Spanish galleon *Montcova*, he per-sonally slaughtered fifty-three officers. His own crew finally mutinied and set him adrift in an open boat without provisions. (The story has a happy ending – two days later, he was rescued by a French ship, but when his identity was discovered, he was put on trial and hanged.)

One pirate's downfall is another's opportu-nity. Henry Avery, the 'King of Pirates', came to be a pirate captain by successfully leading a mutiny in 1694; he was serving as first mate aboard the *Charles* when he and the rest of the crew assumed control while the drunken

⚓ Captain Avery stands before the *Fancy*, which he claimed for himself through mutiny.

⚑ Dissatisfied sailors fighting amongst themselves; divisions within a crew can be extremely costly to a captain.

captain slept. They put him ashore in Africa, renamed the ship *Fancy*, and sailed away to plunder other vessels.

John Gow also became a captain following a particularly bloody mutiny on 3 November 1724 aboard the *George Galley*. Seven men cut the throats of the ship's surgeon, chief mate, and clerk while they slept. The former captain, Oliver Freneau, evaded two mutineers who tried to throw him overboard, only to face a third, who slashed his throat. It took gunpower to finish him off entirely. The mutineers tossed the bodies into the ocean and renamed the ship *Revenge* – a fitting moniker.

William Fly both led a mutiny and fell victim to one in the course of his one-month-long pirate career – the shortest in pirate history. While a bosun aboard a slave ship he killed its captain, renaming the ship *Fame's Revenge* and assuming the role of pirate chief, terrorizing North America's New England coast. Infamous for his outbursts of rage and savage brutality, Fly often whipped his captives with up to one hundred lashes – easily enough to kill a man. His own carelessness brought about his downfall; having sent most of his loyal crew off to attack another ship, he was almost isolated among a majority of hostile crew members, who mutinied and took him prisoner. Fly was gibbeted in Boston Harbour; the story goes that he reproached the hangman for not knowing his craft and fixed the noose around his own neck.

So take heed of my advice, to spare yourself from such treatment at the hands of your crew.

Pirate havens

Aside from effectively managing your crew at sea, one of your main concerns will be finding safe bases and towns in which you can exchange your ill-gotten booty for gold and silver, fine food and strong drink – or whatever you choose! Remember, pirate crews have been known to destroy the (inedible) contents of ships that they have successfully raided if they don't have a guarantee of a safe haven in which to sell them – what a waste. So pirates will band together to establish secret ports in which they can conduct their trade. And you may be surprised to find that the merchants and colonists who publicly denounce you and your fellow pirates are regular customers. Trading with pirates can be a highly profitable enterprise for all parties, especially merchants. This was particularly true in North America before the war of Independence, because of the trade restrictions Britain imposed on its colonies. Of course, pirates do not concern themselves with such regulations, and so a merchant can avoid taxation and fetch a higher price for their wares.

That said, believe it or not, government support is often vital in establishing pirate havens. Do not forget that pirates offer the authorities valuable services, looting the wealth of enemy nations and protecting vulnerable territories distant from the mainland. This is how the first pirate town, Tortuga, on the Caribbean island of the same name, gained prominence – the French government needed buccaneers to protect the isle from her enemies. By the early 1600s, the rocky island had become the stronghold of a motley group of adventurers, thieves and escaped slaves preying on the Spanish treasure ships that passed. The great captain Jean le Vasseur built a castle to help guard the island's harbour. The pirates who flocked to Tortuga organized themselves into a fraternity of thieves called the 'Brethren of the Coast', and developed their own Code of pirate conduct so that what everyone else would call criminal behaviour could flourish.

⚓ Kingston Harbour and Port Royal, Jamaica, once a fine pirate haven.

Similarly, Port Royal in Kingston, Jamaica, one of the most infamous pirate havens during the Golden Age of Piracy, only flourished after the Jamaican authorities declared it safe ground for pirates in exchange for protection from the Spanish. The town soon became a major staging ground for privateers. Early in his career, before his legendary sacking of Panama City, Henry Morgan used Port Royal as a base of operations for raids on the Spanish strongholds of the Caribbean. By the 1660s, its streets were lined with taverns and brothels eager to cater to the tastes of young buccaneers flush with Spanish loot; it was not unknown for a reckless pirate to squander thousands of Spanish *reales* in a single night, sending them into destitution.

Perhaps you intend to make a real splash and set up a pirate base of your own. You'll want to attract the lowest of the low-lifes currently marauding on the Seven Seas. Here, the Pirates' Code should not apply – your crew have restrained themselves at sea, and now is the time for mayhem to rule! Do not concern yourself too much about exerting control over the carrying of weapons; it will get you nowhere. The free exchange of goods and services for money with no questions being asked should be the guiding principle of your economic plan. A safe haven for criminals,

Libertalia: A pirate paradise

According to pirate legend, a group of pioneering thieves left the pirate haven of St. Mary's on Madagascar to set up a utopian colony called Libertalia, where they organized a democratic government, dividing all treasure and cattle equally among themselves. A delegation of pirates met at least once a year to discuss any issues arising within the settlement, maintaining the peace; no action could be taken without their consent. Thomas Tew, a famous pirate captain born in Rhode Island, America, who had once plundered Arabian and Indian cargoes in the Red Sea under the protection of wealthy and influential sponsors, was named admiral

of Libertalia's fleet of ships and was charged with enticing more pirates to join the enclave. He was famously charismatic – a governor of New York, Thomas Fletcher, was dismissed from his post after describing Tew as 'a very pleasant man who tells wonderful stories', deemed to be too friendly with a pirate. But in June 1695, Tew was shot and killed by his intended victims while boarding a prize ship owned by the Great Moghal of India. So dies the legend of Libertalia. No one has ever found any trace of it, so I think it existed only in the imagination of pirates who hoped for a better life one day.

murderers and fraudsters is what any true pirate seeks. He can then rest easy in your little enclave, secure in the knowledge that if he is cheated, robbed or even murdered no one will take the slightest bit of notice.

When setting up your hideaway, it is most important to appraise the suitability of the location. Nassau, on the Bahamian island of New Providence, offers a good role model: sitting at the centre of the trade routes between Europe and the West Indies, it once provided pirates with plenty of ships to prey on, and its proximity to the North American colonies provided markets where they could sell their plunder. Further, the many coves and inlets in the Bahamas were perfect for hiding when pursued, and for safely careening and repairing ships without fearing arrest. Its numerous limestone caverns are convenient hiding places for treasure, while food, fresh water, and wood for repairs are greatly abundant. The hills overlooking the harbour give a clear view for miles, so pirates could spot prospective targets or enemy ships long before the vessels neared the island, giving them ample time to plan their assault. That's why it is commonly said that when a pirate sleeps, he doesn't dream of heaven – he dreams that he has returned to New Providence.

So, carefully lay your plans, capture your town, and it will be a paradise indeed! Though a word of caution: paradise, perhaps, cannot last forever. Take the case of Port Royal, that most rowdy of pirate towns; after Jamaica passed anti-piracy laws in 1687, its 'Gallows Point' became a notorious location of executions, claiming the lives of the infamous 'Calico' Jack Rackham and Charles Vane, among countless other nameless souls. Even New Providence has been lost to the efforts of authorities to quell pirate activity in Bahamian waters; in 1718, amid rising fear that the rampant pirate activity in the Bahamas was becoming a threat to the colony, Governor Rogers offered a pardon to any pirate who surrendered, and executed a band of convicted pirates in Nassau. From then on, to the horror of us all, New Providence was slowly transformed into one of the main headquarters for anti-piracy operations in the Caribbean – pirate heaven turned to pirate hell.

8

The Pirate in Old Age

Of course, you will be hoping for a long and lucrative career of plundering and pillaging, but – assuming you do not fall to another pirate's cutlass or the gallows – you must prepare yourself for your pirate retirement. Fear not; it has been my experience that everyone loves an old pirate. Indeed, since I hung up my pistols, there have been few nights in the tavern when I have had to purchase my own drink; there will always be someone who wants to hear my tales and inspect my scars. You will be similarly war-worn and fascinating. If you have never owned a parrot, now is the time to buy one. Teach it to say 'Pieces of Eight!' and you will never have to pay for a beer again. But first, of course, you must make it to old age…

A price on your head

I have been very fortunate to survive the seas; not everyone is as lucky as I am. As a pirate, you will be wanted not only by the official authorities – the local watch, the excisemen – but also by opportunistic bounty hunters who reckon they can make smart money by handing you over. Just read the words of an official proclamation issued in Virginia in 1719: 'upon the conviction, or making due proof of the killing of all, and every such pirate the bounty hunter will be rewarded as follows':

Blackbeard himself £100

Other pirate commanders £40

Pirate lieutenant, master, bosun, carpenter etc £20

All inferior officers £15

Private men £10

So you see, while the most famously villainous pirates earn the highest price, ordinary pirates have a bounty on their heads as well. So best to watch your back at all times. Follow the

⚓ The death of Blackbeard, one of the most wanted pirates, at the hands of Lieutenant Robert Maynard and his crew.

example of Captain Peter Easton, a privateer of the English Crown, whose claim to fame is that he was never defeated by anyone commissioned to hunt him down. His vast and powerful fleet counted forty ships and over 1,500 men at the height of his power, so you can imagine the attention he drew. Peter's most significant victory came in 1610 in Newfoundland, Canada, when he attacked Sir Richard Whitbourne's fleet and defeated thirty ships. Easton took Whitbourne himself captive upon his ship, hoping to convert him to the pirate creed as a powerful partner, but even after eleven weeks of lavish treatment on board Whitbourne refused to be swayed, remaining firmly loyal to the Crown – though he did offer to petition for Easton's pardon, a promise he duly fulfilled upon his release.

A pirate's penalty

Perhaps you think the risk of being caught is worth the rewards you can reap from your life of marauding. Maybe you should consider what will happen to you if you *are* apprehended before making such a bold declaration! Of course, it is no secret, and little surprise. Seamen and their families are well aware of the penalty for piracy – the publicity surrounding the trials and executions of pirates makes sure of that. A pirate trial is always popular in the newspapers and broadsheets, the speeches and confessions of criminals about to be hanged in England and the colonies being gleefully printed and circulated. Newspaper publishers know they can rely on large sales in the days following an execution.

Let's begin with the best-case scenario. In 1718, as part of the efforts by the British government to stamp out piracy altogether, a general amnesty was granted to all pirates if they agreed to give up their lawless ways forever. Several particularly self-interested captains took advantage of it and went on to become pirate hunters themselves – the ultimate betrayal of the Pirates' Code! But not all pirates can abandon their roots

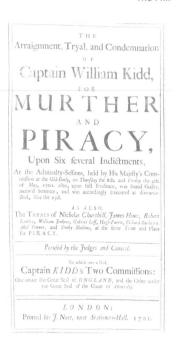

THE

Arraignment, Tryal, and Condemnation

OF

Captain William Kidd,

FOR

MURTHER

AND

PIRACY,

Upon Six feveral Indictments,

At the Admiralty-Seffions, held by His Majefty's Commiffion at the *Old-Baily*, on *Thurfday* the 8th. and *Friday* the 9th. of *May*, 1701. who, upon full Evidence, was found Guilty, receiv'd Sentence, and was accordingly Executed at *Execution-Dock*, *May* the 23d.

AS ALSO,

The TRYALS of *Nicholas Churchill, James Howe, Robert Lamley, William Jenkins, Gabriel Loff, Hugh Parrot, Richard Barlicorn, Abel Owens,* and *Darby Mullins,* at the fame Time and Place for PIRACY.

Perufed by the Judges and Council.

To which are added,

Captain *KIDD*'s Two Commiffions:

One under the Great Seal of *ENGLAND,* and the Other under the Great Seal of the Court of *Admiralty.*

LONDON:

Printed for *J. Nutt,* near *Stationers-Hall.* 1701.

◄◄ Broadsheet advertising the trial of Captain William Kidd. That it also advertises his condemnation should give you an idea of how well you could hope to fare at trial!

so easily; Blackbeard accepted the pardon, but returned to piracy later that same year. It has also happened that pirates receive individual pardons; convicted pirates can repent of their crimes and ask for mercy, and may even find sympathetic souls willing to help them with their case, such as Peter Easton found in Richard Whitbourne – though Easton in fact chose to ignore the pardon once granted, instead sailing on to the Barbary Coast to try his hand at piracy there. Of course, some pirates, and especially those in dire straits, already captured by the Crown, are more grateful for such good Samaritans. When Black Sam Bellamy's crew were put on trial in Boston in 1717, a clergyman called Cotton Mather regularly met the men in prison during their incarceration, and even appealed on their behalf during the trial. He argued successfully in court that Thomas Davis, the carpenter of the *Whydah*, was an honest seaman who had been pressed into service by Bellamy's crew because they needed his specialist skills. The court accepted his argument and Davis walked free. It is not always so straightforward: six other crew members who Mather represented were hanged, in spite of his efforts and their repentance. You may not even be granted a trial – one of Bellamy's captured crew was a Miskito Indian called John Julian. Like so many other arrested black or Native American pirates, he was sold straight into slavery.

⚓ The 1717 trial of the surviving crew of the *Whydah*, represented by Cotton Mather.

Of course, not all pirates will feel remorse for their crimes. Thomas Morris, hanged in the Bahamas in 1718, was equally defiant, saying that he wished only that he had been 'a greater plague to these islands'. In 1726, Cotton Mather tried to persuade the notorious pirate William Fly to repent. He declined, and when he stood on the gallows he made a bold and unrepentant statement: that merchant captains were responsible for piracy, driving honest seamen to it by mistreating them and refusing to pay them on time. He was not alone in this philosophy; Captain Johnson tells the story of how Black Sam Bellamy caught up with a sloop under the command of a man called Captain Beer, who refused to join Bellamy and his crew because of his responsibilities as the captain of a privately owned merchantman. Bellamy thought the captain was a hypocrite to serve rich men who robbed the poor just as much as any pirate, and was scornful of the man's pride:

the cowardly whelps have not the courage otherwise to defend what they get
by knavery; but damn ye altogether: damn them for a pack of crafty rascals,

and you, who serve them, for a parcel of hen-hearted numbskulls. They vilify us, the scoundrels do, when there is only this difference: they rob the poor under the cover of law, forsooth, and we plunder the rich under the protection of our own courage.

Self-righteous claims such as this will not get you very far when you are arrested and put on trial, however. Most pirate trials last no more than one or two days, even when twenty or thirty prisoners are involved. This is generally because there are no arguments provided on your behalf. It is the usual practice for the accused men to conduct their own defence, and as most pirates are seamen with little or no education they struggle to make a good case for themselves. Their response to questioning is usually one of the following: they say nothing at all; they say they were drunk at the time; or they claim they were forced into the deeds they stand accused of – that their ships had been captured by pirates and they had been compelled to join the crew.

Plan your defence: a lawyer's advice

You are unlikely to have a Cotton Mather to argue on your behalf, so I have consulted a senior defence lawyer who has acted on behalf of several former colleagues of mine. Most of his clients found his advice useful, even though they were hanged anyway. He agreed to supply the following statement, which may be of use to you:

I have acted on behalf of several very prominent gentlemen of the seas over a period of many years, and I am grateful to my friend X for allowing me the opportunity to pass on some of my legal knowledge to a new generation. I must point out first of all that my comments can only apply to the laws of England, and refer specifically to privateers who have been commissioned by

His Majesty's Government. It cannot be overstated that a privateer acting on behalf of His Majesty who is captured by the French or Spanish can expect no mercy and no redress. To them, he will always be a criminal, and will most certainly be hanged.

The specific situations I have in mind are those when an honest privateer is apprehended by the authorities and charged with being a common pirate. My advice to clients is always to claim two forms of defence: first, that they are acting under the protection of Letters of Marque (which should be produced on request), and second, that everything that they have done has been motivated by a keen sense of patriotism to His Majesty the King. The latter statement will demonstrate the purity of one's motives and should be sufficient to soften the heart of even the coldest presiding magistrate.

Problems will only arise when the activity for which a client has been arrested has involved attacks upon shipping actually owned by His Majesty the King. As abundant case law has shown, the crucial phrase in any Letter of Marque is 'His Majesty's enemies' not, as Lord Chief Justice Smithers once wittily remarked, 'His Majesty's friends'. French, Spanish, American and even Scottish (under certain circumstances) shipping are legitimate targets. Ships owned by the East India Company are not.

Be wary – I have heard prosecuting counsel attempting to pull the wool over the eyes of a presiding magistrate by accepting at face value the service to His Majesty the King and the patriotic fervour earlier expounded by the defendant, thus lulling them into a false sense of security. A particularly aggressive lawyer will then try to convince the court that the defendant did not attack ships in order to further the noble aims for which he was assigned, but that the reverse was true: that he accepted Letters of Marque in order to attack ships and increase his own personal wealth.

In one particularly sorry case I defended, the prosecuting counsel read from the Letter of Marque issued to the defendant that his role was, I quote, 'to demoralize the French people and destroy its merchant fleet'. He asked the jury to consider whether or not the defendant was carrying out those duties, either in the letter or the spirit of the law, when he was arrested in Plymouth *with thirty barrels of brandy stolen from a ship belonging to the Duke of Northampton. 'Is the Duke of Northampton a Frenchman?' he asked, amid great glee. 'If he is not, gentlemen of the jury, then I suggest to you that the defendant has exceeded his Letters of Marque, and is a common pirate, and as such should be hanged'. The jury agreed with him and the defendant was sentenced to be executed. He appealed, and it was pointed out that the Duke of Northampton's ancestors had come over with the Norman Invasion in 1066, so technically speaking he was, therefore, a Frenchman. The judge at the Court of Appeal took the point, but dismissed it on the grounds that whatever dubious ancestry the Duke may have possessed, he was not the King's enemy and therefore fell outside the accepted definition.*

My overall advice to you is this: stress the legality of your commission, and the intense patriotism that motivated its acceptance. Never, never, attack a friendly ship, and never give the impression that you chose the privateer's life for money. (In short, become a good liar, and fast!)

I hope my distinguished friend's comments will be helpful in your defence, if ever necessary. If the need to demonstrate the purity of one's motives alarms you, know that you are not alone. The privateer Basil Ringrose certainly raided ships for personal gain, as he explains in his journal. After an especially long and fruitless voyage, his fellow crewmen, disappointed that they had so little to show for their troubles, decided to attack Panama, writing: 'our great expectations of taking a huge booty of gold at this place being totally vanished, we were unwilling to have come so far for nothing ... Hereupon we resolved to go to Panama, [in] which place, if we could take [it], we were assured we should get treasure enough to satisfy our hungry appetite for gold and riches'. Somehow, I do not think Mr Ringrose would have lasted long in a court of law.

Guilty!

So you've been declared guilty. What now?

For many years, English pirates have been hanged at Execution Dock on the north bank of the Thames, condemned men being paraded across London Bridge and past the Tower of London to a bend of the river at Wapping. The gallows are set up on the shore near the low-tide mark. When an execution is due to take place, large crowds will gather on the shore and in boats moored out in the river – such a spectacle is not to be missed. Depending on the pirate's notoriety, the body may be taken away to be buried in an unmarked grave or sent to Surgeon's Hall for dissection, or displayed at a prominent point on the river, so that it can be seen by the crews of all ships entering and leaving the port – a grisly reminder of the fate of any person who turns to piracy. To make sure the corpse remains intact for as long as possible, it is coated with tar to stop birds from pecking at the flesh. The body is then fitted into a gibbet – a specially made harness of iron hoops and chains that holds the head, body and legs in place. The body of Captain Kidd was left suspended in this way for more than twenty years at Tilbury Point, on the lower reaches of the Thames. His remains would have been visible for an hour or more as ships navigated Sea Reach, the broad stretch of the river that curves around the lonely point. Hangings like this are still the norm in London, and the Piracy Act, passed by the English Parliament in 1698, has also made it possible for admirals to conduct trials at sea or in any foreign port, so that the accused does not even have be brought to England to face justice. It has led to the execution of some 600 pirates, estimated to be around ten per cent of those once active in the Caribbean.

⚓ The execution of Captain James Lowry at Execution Dock, London, in 1752. This was the fate that awaited scores of pirates whose names are now lost to history.

← The body of Captain WIlliam Kidd, left gibbeted at Tilbury Point for twenty years to serve as a vivid warning of the consequences of piracy.

Of course, the execution doesn't always go to plan; part of the draw for the crowd is that a pirate execution can be a very theatrical affair. When John Gow was hanged in 1726, the rope broke; Gow picked himself up, casually brushed down his clothes and climbed the ladder for the second attempt. In 1727, a sympathetic crowd in Kingston, Jamaica, over-ruled the magistrates who had sentenced a local pirate who was very popular. The mob took the law into their own hands and rescued the man from the gallows. And Blackbeard once threatened to burn Boston to the ground if Bellamy's men were hanged – though as it turned out these were empty words.

Calling it quits

You don't fancy the bother of a trial, or the risk of meeting the gallows? Good news! Pirates have been known to live fulfilling lives after voluntarily turning aside from their nefarious pursuits. The best example is Lancelot Blackburne (1658–1743), an Englishman said to have been involved with buccaneers on the Caribbean island of Nevis in his youth, possibly acting as their chaplain. Despite his time among this decidedly impious crowd, Blackburne returned to England to rise to the rank of Archbishop of York. Then there is 'Red Legs' Greaves, a Scottish buccaneer who captured the island of Margarita, off the coast of Venezuela, in 1675. This raid made him rich enough to retire from piracy, and he settled down to the calmer life of a gentleman farmer – until he was recognized by one of his former victims. Imprisoned in the dungeon of Port Royal, he awaited his execution, but in 1692 the town was hit by an earthquake, and as one of the few survivors he made his escape. Evidently shaken by the experience, and a truly reformed man, he became a pirate hunter and earned himself a royal pardon. In later life he even became a philanthropist, giving to charities and public institutions – quite the about-turn from his former occupation.

Perhaps you'd rather sink into obscurity and live out the rest of your days without any of your new neighbours knowing about your sordid past. In that case, you might want to imitate Dixie Bull. Once an honest trapper trading for furs in Penobscot Bay, Maine, he resorted to piracy in 1623 after French buccaneers seized all of his provisions, leaving him destitute – in fact, he is regarded by many as the first American pirate. He persuaded a gang of fishermen, traders and seamen to join him in targeting merchant vessels and trading posts along the New England coast, provoking the attention of the authorities, who sent five vessels on an expedition against him. Bull (wisely) disappeared from the New England area in 1633, and was never heard of again. Rumours abound about where he ended up; some claimed that he had joined the French, while others speculated that he had returned to his native England. According to one popular poem, Dixie was killed in a sword fight. We'll probably never know his true fate – which is no doubt just how he wanted it.

Renouncing or disguising your previous piratehood does not guarantee you a peaceful death, however. Many an ex-pirate has succumbed to some exotic illness picked up on their travels, or otherwise deteriorated due to the hazards of the pirate lifestyle. Perhaps the most famous buccaneer to die of natural causes was the great Sir Henry Morgan, who developed dropsy, a peculiar and painful condition whereby fluid accumulates between cavities in the body and the skin – the result of being 'much given to drinking and sitting up late', according to his physician. So you see, it is possible for even the most famous of pirates to go out with a whimper, not a bang.

Death at sea

Now for some bad news. Though it is important to be aware of the risk of hanging, relatively few ordinary pirates meet an unpleasant end by being executed; many more die from fighting, disease or drowning – ultimately, you are most likely to die at sea. If you die in the midst of a battle, your body might just be tossed over the side by your distracted crewmates. Otherwise, crews perform simple ceremonies as soon as time permits – pirates, like other seamen, prefer not to have corpses on their ships owing to the health hazard they are believed to pose. Further, preserving bodies involves the use of alcohol – and why waste good spirits on the dead? When the time comes, you will be given a rudimentary funeral and consigned to the ocean. According to tradition, your body will be placed in your hammock, and two cannonballs placed

A group of sailors performs the simple ceremonies due for the departed before sending his body to Davy Jones' Locker.

at your feet. (These are believed to prevent departed sailors from following the ship.) The sailmaker will sew thirteen stitches to close the hammock, with last stitch piercing your nose; this guarantees that you are truly dead. Some of your comrades will share happy memories, and a prayer might be spoken before your body is slid off a plank into the watery depths. If you have a family, your crew might auction off your belongings and give some of the profits to your next of kin.

The pirate who dies at sea is said to have gone to a place called 'Davy Jones' Locker' – that is, the bottom of the sea. In 1751, Tobias Smollett, a Scottish author and poet, wrote, 'This same Davy Jones, according to sailors, is the fiend that presides over all the evil spirits of the deep, and is often seen in various shapes, perching among the rigging on the eve of hurricanes, ship-wrecks, and other disasters to which sea-faring life is exposed, warning the devoted wretch of death and woe'. Many a pirate will end their perilous career by joining those who have preceded them to Davy Jones' Locker.

Buried treasure – the pirate pension

You may, of course, beat the odds and avoid all such unpleasantness, in which case, congratulations! You may now retire to dry land to enjoy the wealth that your endeavours have brought you. Henry Avery, who became a pirate captain through mutiny, leading to his renown as one of the most feared and successful pirates of the Red Sea, didn't take many ships in the course of his career, but the two that he did capture were among the finest in the Indian Ocean. One was an Indian treasure ship, laden to the gunwales with gold and jewels, more than sufficient to support his retirement – and to attract the attention of various bounty and treasure hunters. Clever Avery managed to keep his true whereabouts concealed until the time of his death. Ideally, you will have amassed similarly considerable wealth, having controlled any impulses to drink or gamble it all away – and crucially, like Avery, you will have stopped any other nefarious pirates from getting their hands on it, and you.

But how? You may not feel that you can trust your crew, and there aren't many decent hiding places on a ship. You may have heard stories about pirates burying their treasure. Well, it's certainly an idea, and I do know of one pirate, a Frenchman called Dulaien, who hid a vast amount of treasure in various places on land before his ship was searched. He then took a long, leisurely time spending his fortune, but I don't think Monsieur Dulaien actually buried any of it in the ground. Captain Kidd is known to have buried some treasure shortly before he was arrested (though this backfired, as it was found and used against him as evidence during his trial), and in fact many ordinary civilians bury money in their gardens anyway. So bury your treasure if you must – but make sure you remember where you buried it, and that nobody else knows. You will have read stories about pirates drawing a treasure map and marking with an 'X' the spot where the treasure is buried. But does that really seem like a smart idea?

Pyle illustrates Captain Kidd overseeing the burial of his treasure by two of his most trusted crew.

Remember, the whole essence of buried treasure is secrecy. Blackbeard must have amassed great wealth, but when he died, all that was found when his last locations were searched were stashes of cocoa, sugar, cotton and indigo. Where was the gold? Common speculation has it that it lies on one of the islands off North America's Carolinas. Will anyone ever find it? Legend tells that Blackbeard was once asked if anyone knew where his treasure was buried. He replied, 'Only two people know where the treasure lies; the Devil and myself, and he who lives the longest may claim it all'.

9
The Last Word

So, my friend, you have completed the pirate's training manual! There is little more that any book-learning can teach you. From now on, you must learn on the job, once you take up your first position on a pirate ship. So good luck to you, but first, a final note of warning.

As you have surely gathered by now, we pirates are not exactly popular individuals. Most of us have a price on our heads, of course, and the hangman awaits for anyone who is caught by the Royal Navy, but there is danger too from within our own ranks – all pirates have rivals. We carve out our own piece of territory in which to operate, but there will always be others who wish to take it from us. Many a good shipmate of mine has been murdered by a jealous rival, so watch your back at all times, because no one knows when a murderer might

A note from the Editor

S o ends the manuscript of *Pirate: The Buccaneer's Manual* by an
unknown 'gentleman of the seas', as he terms himself. There has
been much speculation over his true identity and, of course, that of
his murderer. Although there is no definite proof as to who the 'gentleman'
was, the book contains a few tantalizing clues. The author refers on several
occasions to Bartholomew Roberts in quite familiar terms, and even claims
an acquaintance at second hand through his father. He also seems to be
particularly knowledgeable about the coastline of New England and the
Carolinas, probably making several transatlantic voyages himself, suggesting a strong American connection, though his ultimate loyalty is evidently
to the English Crown. He refers to the American War of Independence and
also to the death of the privateer John Paul Jones in 1792, which occurred
not long before the author's own death. Most fascinating of all is his deep
knowledge of the history of piracy around the world. That alone suggests
that he was an educated man, and very well read. He refers to Captain
Johnson's famous *A General History of the Robberies and Murders of the most
notorious Pyrates*, which was first published in 1724, but his learning clearly
extends far beyond that popular work, and the most remarkable aspect
of that wider knowledge concerns the pirates of China and Japan. The
former were quite well known, but during the eighteenth century Japan
was a closed country, so the only source from which the author could have
obtained any information would have been through the Dutch trading post

on the island of Dejima in Nagasaki Bay. That place acted as a conduit for information to the benefit of both Holland and Japan, and the author has clearly benefited from the information that was sent home. I have furnished his account with illustrations of the lands he might have visited, the sights he might have seen and some of the scoundrels with whom he may have rubbed shoulders.

There is no question about when the manuscript was written: the year 1793 is stated in its introduction. Court records show that its author was murdered sometime during October 1794. Yet still we have no name, so his true identity will forever remain a mystery – as will that of the man who is presumed to have murdered him while our author wrote the concluding page of this remarkable book. All we know for certain is that the incident occurred in a lodging house in Chatham, England, which burned down shortly after the murder. As the victim was a seafarer, an enquiry was launched by the Admiralty, and a brief report is preserved in the National Archives (*Calendar of State Papers 1794: Report by the Board of the Admiralty into the Most Grievous Murder that has recently occurred at Chatham*). The report is formal and largely uninteresting, apart from the following paragraph, relating the testimony given before the Court by the owner of the lodging house:

> *He was a very private gentlemen who kept himself to himself. He rarely spoke and his accent was very unusual, possibly American. He always paid his rent on time and used Spanish doubloons to do so, to which I had no objection. Most of the time he stayed in his room writing, and always required me to serve his meals there. Otherwise you always knew when he was moving about the house, on account of his peg leg. He never had any visitors and his only friend appeared to be his parrot. On the night of the murder I was asleep and heard*

nothing, so I presume the murderer got in through the window, which was still open when I took his breakfast up the following morning and found the body slumped over the book he had been writing. Nothing in the room had been disturbed, apart from his sea chest. It had been wrenched open, and evidently the murderer had removed from it a small wooden casket, which now lay on the floor. I had never seen it before. It was empty, and written on the lid were the words 'Treasure Map'. The murderer must have stolen it.

The Board of the Admiralty returned a verdict of murder by an unknown hand, and there the matter ended. The bloodstained manuscript of the *Manual* was later presented by the Admiralty to the library of the British Museum in 1797, and it remains in the Manuscript Collection of the British Library to this day. The *Manual* was published in a small octavo volume in 1811 but only three copies are known to exist. The one owned by Cambridge University Library has provided the basis for this edition.

There is a curious epilogue to the story, mentioned in an article in *The Times* in June 1830. Under the headline 'The Chatham Murder of 1794 – An Antiquarian Investigates', the anonymous author draws our attention to certain evidence drawn from Parish Registers. His research confirms that the lodging house in which the murder took place was indeed consumed by a mysterious fire shortly after the incident, and that the owner is soon afterwards listed in a different Parish Register at the address of a rich and imposing stately home in Sussex with extensive landownings. There is no reference to the missing treasure map, nor the missing parrot.

Newfoundland

Lond·
BRITAIN
Plymouth
St Malo

·New York

ATLANTIC

Charleston· NASSAU   OCEAN   Alg

↓TORTUGA
↙ HISPANIOLA

PACIFIC   ← JAMAICA

OCEAN   ·Cartagena
Panama City

UNOFFICIAL
MAP
OF THE
WORLD

RUSSIA

INNOSHIMA

KURUSHIMA   JAPAN

NOSHIMA

Istanbul

CHINA

INDIA

Ayutthaya

I N D I A N

O C E A N

MADAGASCAR

Cape of Good Hope

Timeline

700 BC   King Sennacherib, ruler of the Neo-Assyrian empire, fights pirates in the Persian Gulf.

330 BC   Alexander the Great campaigns to clear pirates from the Mediterranean seas.

67 BC   Pirates target Roman grain supplies supplying the city of Delos in the Greek Cyclades.

AD 310   King Shapur II of Persia fights pirates in the Persian Gulf.

1243   King Henry III of England issues the first official privateering commission to Adam Robernolt and William le Sauvage.

1492   Christopher Columbus lands in North America, marking the beginning of Spanish exploitation of the New World.

1518   Aroudj Barbarossa dies in battle.

1529   Kheir ed-Din Barbarossa, continuing his brother's legacy, captures Algiers, stamping out the Spanish presence along the Barbary Coast.

1535   Barbary corsairs launch a legendary attack on Port Mahon, Menorca.

1546   Kheir ed-Din Barbarossa dies peacefully in his coastal palace in Constantinople (now Istanbul).

1556   Chinese pirates Xu Hai and Wang Zhi lead their *wako* crew on a campaign in China's Zhejiang province.

1580	Sir Francis Drake returns home to England, completing his three-year voyage around the world.
1581–86	*Wako* raids against Spanish colonies in the Philippines.
1600	Founding of the pirate haven Tortuga in the Caribbean.
1604	Murakami Takeyoshi dies.
1610	English privateer Peter Easton defeats a fleet of thirty ships in Newfoundland, Canada.
1623	Javanese pirates attack Ayutthaya, capital of Siam, but are turned back by a fierce resistance of Japanese pirates armed with cannon-loaded elephants.
	Dixie Bull turns to piracy, to mysteriously vanish ten years later.
1650	Start of Golden Age of Piracy.
1655	Buccaneers hired by English colonists expel the Spanish from Jamaica.
1660	Heyday of Port Royal, Jamaica.
1662	Zheng Chenggong captures Taiwan, dies of malaria shortly afterwards.
1671	Captain Henry Morgan leads the sack of Panama.
	Stenka Razin put to death in Moscow.
1672	Captain Henry Morgan 'arrested' by the English authorities.
1675	Scottish buccaneers 'Red Legs' Greaves captures Margarita, off the coast of Venezuela.
1683	Dutch Captain Van Hoorn leads 1,000 in a raid on Veracruz, Mexico.
1692	Earthquake in Port Royal, Jamaica, frees the imprisoned 'Red Legs' Greaves.

1693	English privateers send a fireship into the French base of St Malo, but it fizzles.
1694	Englishman Henry Avery becomes a pirate captain by instigating mutiny on the *Charles*.
1695	Captain Thomas Tew, who according to legend founded the pirate base Libertalia, killed while attempting a raid on Indian ships.
1696	Scotsman William Kidd terrorizes the seas of West Africa.
1698	Piracy Act passed by English parliament, enabling sailors to be accused and tried in foreign ports.
1701	William Kidd hanged and gibbetted.
1711	French corsair Réné Duguay-Trouin captures Rio de Janeiro.
1713	Benjamin Horngold establishes a pirate base at New Providence.
1715	Thousands of English sailors dismissed from the Royal Navy after the War of the Spanish Succession ends.
1717	Captain Black Sam Bellamy captures the *Whydah Gally*, renaming it simply the *Whydah*, in the Caribbean.
1718	Blackbeard blockades Charlestown, and is pursued and killed by the Royal Navy's Lieutenant Robert Maynard.
	Pirate haven New Providence is closed down.
	Pirate amnesty proclaimed by the British government.
	Stede Bonnet and his crew hanged in Charleston, USA.
1720	'Calico Jack' Rackham hanged, but his female accomplices, Anne Bonny and Mary Read, are spared.
1722	Bartholomew Roberts ('Black Bart') is killed in battle.
1721	Edward Low mutinies and starts piracy.

1724   Ned Low's crew mutiny and maroon him; he is 'rescued' by a French ship, only to be hanged when the French authorities learn his true identity.

Captain Johnson's *A General History of the Robberies and Murders of the most notorious Pyrates* published.

John Gow becomes a pirate captain after leading a bloody mutiny aboard the *George Galley*.

1730   End of Golden Age of Piracy.

1736   Act of Indemnity for Smugglers enacted by English Parliament.

1776   John Paul Jones commands Providence.

1779   John Paul Jones, so-called 'Father of the US navy', captures the British *Serapis* in the Battle of Flamborough Head.

1789   American pirate Rachel Wall is executed, becoming the last woman to be hanged in Massachusetts.

1793   Completion of *Pirate: The Buccaneer's Manual* (and death of the unknown author).

Further Reading

For accessible and reliable illustrated information about historical pirates, Angus Konstam's *Pirate: The Golden Age* (Osprey Warrior, 2011), which tells in words and vivid pictures the true story of how pirates behaved and looked, is a good place to start. *The Pirate Ship 1660-1730* (Osprey New Vanguard, 2003), by the same author, gives good detail on the types of vessels commandeered by pirates, while Réné Chartrand's *The Spanish Main 1492-1800* (Osprey Fortress, 2006) offers a detailed account of the forts and castles along this hotbed of pirate activity.

An excellent book offering insight into the reality of piracy from the point of view of law and order is Peter Earle's *The Pirate Wars* (Methuen, 2004), which describes how various navies tried to drive pirates from the seas.

Robert E. Lee's *Blackbeard the Pirate: A Reappraisal of His Life and Times* (Blair, 1974) is a very good account of its subject grounded firmly in historical research, while Benerson Little's *The Sea Rover's Practice: Pirate Tactics and Techniques 1630-1730* (Potomac Books, 2007) is a treasure trove of highly detailed information on its subject gleaned from contemporary accounts and is probably the best book to read (after this one) if you wish to learn more about the practical side of piracy.

Captain Johnson's *A General History of the Robberies and Murders of the most notorious Pyrates*, the primary resource for many pirate biographies, also remains widely available in various formats.

Picture Credits

145   Bancroft Library, University of California, Berkeley

148   *Howard Pyle's Book of Pirates*, 1921

149   *The Pirates' Own Book*, by Charles Ellms, 1834

150   Historical Picture Archive/Corbis

151   Alamy Stock Photo/Chronicle

152   *Howard Pyle's Book of Pirates*, 1921

153   Getty Images/Bettmann

154   Universal Images Group

156   Mary Evans Picture Library

157   Culture Club

158   Private Collection/Look and Learn

161   Library of Congress, Washington, D.C.

165   Diomedia/British Library, London

167   Library of Congress, Washington, D.C.

177   Interfoto

179   Larry Stevens Coinpicks

Index

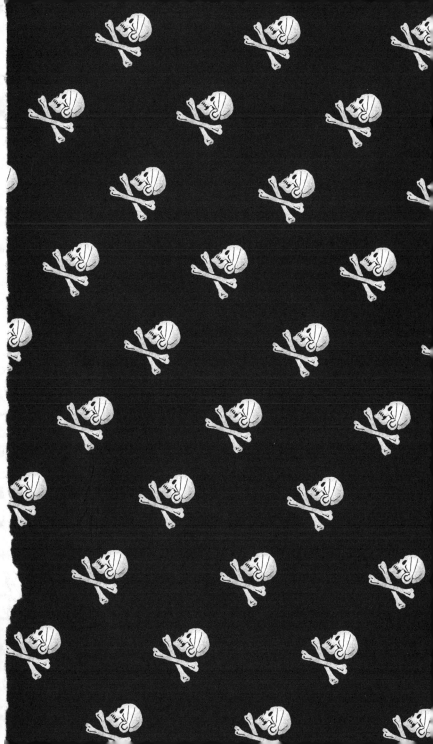